D0778855

Private Urban Renewal

Private Urban Renewal

A Different Residential Trend

Eileen Zeitz
Center for Municipal and
Metropolitan Research of the
National Capital Area

Lexington Books
D.C. Heath and Company
Lexington, Massachusetts
Toronto

Library of Congress Cataloging in Publication Data

Zeitz, Eileen.
    Private urban renewal.

    Bibliography: p. 000
    Includes index.
    1. Urban renewal—United States. 2. Urban renewal—Washington,
D.C. 3. Housing—United States. 4. Housing—Washington, D.C. I. Title.
HT175.Z44   309.2'62'09753   78-19568
ISBN 0-669-02627-1

Published simultaneously in Canada

Printed in the United States of America

International Standard Book Number: 0-669-02627-1

Library of Congress Catalog Card Number: 78-19568

Contents

Contents

List of Figures
and Tables

Preface and Acknowledgments

The issue of racial integration has been one of the most persistent difficulties in the United States. This problem has manifested in all areas of functioning and certainly has been particularly problematic in the area of housing. In addition, providing decent housing for the general populace has been a persistent problem—and one that transcends racial considerations. As a nation, we have spent enormous amounts of money on a variety of renewal programs, and the result is that we have managed to reduce rather than to increase the availability of low-cost housing in the nation's cities. Housing problems of the poor and of minority groups remain unsolved. For a time it appeared that inner cities would become "dumping grounds" for these groups. Now something new is occurring in certain areas of inner cities across the country. Certain neighborhoods are experiencing the process of private urban renewal. For a certain amount of time in the course of this process social, economic, and racial housing integration exists by virtue of the definition of the situation. That is, while transition is actively occurring, both the old residents and the new incoming population live side by side. If city governments were able to act quickly, it might be possible to retain heterogeneity in these areas. However, this requires serious commitment to the idea of diversity as a positive value both on the part of federal and local governments as well as the general populace. The process of private urban renewal has been generally neglected to date, and there is some question as to its consequences for the cities in which it is occurring. Where attention has been focused on the process, there is much debate about its significance, its size, and its future potential growth.

It is difficult to examine a new phenomenon. There are many aspects of the process that are not included in this book, and it may raise as many questions as it answers. Therefore this examination must be considered exploratory rather than definitive. It is hoped that it will generate further examination of private urban renewal in other cities across the country.

Many people have assisted in the preparation of this manuscript. To acknowledge all is impossible. However, I must thank Muriel Cantor and Jürg Siegenthaler of the Sociology Department of the American University and John Helmer of the Sociology Department of George Washington University for their time and their ideas. This year I have had the experience of working with many practitioners in their various capacities concerning urban affairs. Their insights and perspectives have been of great value. I have been aided in analysis and directed to data sources by Colin Walters, Senior Consulting Associate at the Center for Municipal and Metropolitan Research of the National Capital Area; Konrad Perlman, Acting Director of Planning and Evaluation, District of Columbia Department of Housing and Community Development; and Henry H. Leland,

Research Division of the United Planning Organization. The Statistical Staff at the Municipal Planning Office of the District of Columbia Government were extremely helpful and provided me with access to current data that otherwise I might not have located. Susan Soucek spent vast amounts of time discussing ideas and editing my work. Nancine Hughes deserves special thanks for typing at great speed and with great accuracy. Without her assistance this manuscript could not have been completed on time. This research was partially funded by a grant-in-aid from Sigma Xi, The Scientific Research Society of North America.

1

Introduction

The purpose of this book is to examine a new urban phenomenon described as private urban renewal of the inner city. The process of private urban renewal is referred to in a number of ways. It is called "reinvasion," "reverse blockbusting," and "urban revitalization." The British refer to the process as gentrification. The term *private urban renewal* seems to be the most appropriate, because it differentiates the process from a variety of other types of efforts being made to salvage the nation's cities. Moreover, the terms reverse blockbusting and reinvasion are misleading because, although the process resembles both of these phenomena, it is different enough to demand unique identity.

Rehabilitation means to restore to a former capacity. In the case of housing, rehabilitation or restoration implies taking a single building or even an entire area of buildings that have fallen into the category of economic liability and turning them into economic assets. This process, when occurring in the public domain, is known as urban renewal. The distinction between private and public urban renewal, or what is generally termed urban renewal, is significant. The U.S. Housing Act of 1954 provided for the rehabilitation of salvageable housing and fully nonresidential land-use projects.[1] Subsequent legislation amplified and enforced public commitment to renewal and enlarged the area of attack from block projects to the entire neighborhood and to the city.[2] Under the terms of these Acts either federal or local funding, or both, are committed and involved in the renewal. Because of the type of funding involved, some control is maintained by the federal and/or local government. This is not the case of private urban renewal, which is not included in the legislation.

Another distinction is that public urban renewal usually guarantees that after the project is completed, a certain amount of low- or moderate-income housing remains in the area. The displaced population is usually far larger than the proportion of the population provided for once renewal is completed, but public urban renewal does guarantee some degree of heterogeneity of population in any given area.[3] Private urban renewal is different because the money spent is privately controlled. There are no federal or local funds that make the renewal possible, nor is there any guarantee of mortgage loans. Another difference is that public urban renewal usually encompasses large areas. The process of private urban renewal usually is undertaken on a more limited scale. Moreover, critics of public urban renewal have argued that it is destructive to the sense of community that exists before the process begins, and private urban renewal appears to have a reverse effect.[4] That is, a sense of commitment and community spirit appears to emerge as the process develops.

Private urban renewal here defined involves several aspects: change in residential land use, building restoration and rehabilitation, real estate speculation, social and ethnic change, changes in zoning, and government involvement and/or lack of involvement. Private urban renewal also involves various participants: realtors, speculators, formal organizations, and varied governmental agencies and officials. Generally the area or district of the city undergoing private urban renewal is upgraded economically, and higher-income groups belonging principally to the white middle class replace the poor, often nonwhite population in the inner city. Thus, dramatically different socioeconomic groupings and sociocultural milieu are created.

The process of private urban renewal appears to represent a type of residential mobility that is running counter to the movement of the white middle class to the suburbs over at least the last two generations.[5] It also questions the many predictions that the central cities of the nation's great metropolitan areas will eventually become lower class, largely Negro slums.[6]

Although most major cities in the United States appear to be experiencing this process, urban sociologists generally have neglected the phenomenon. There is evidence to suggest that it is occurring in Baltimore, Boston, Charleston, and Washington, D.C. A recent report isolates forty-four cities where this process is being reported.[7] The U.S. Senate has recently held hearings to discuss the potential consequences of this process.[8] However, most information regarding the process is available through nonsociological sources.[9] Lack of emphasis on private urban renewal to date is not totally unjustified. That is, until recently the pattern of urban dynamics appeared to be going in a unidirectional manner heading toward further deterioration of inner cities. The most recent history of cities indicates that they have experienced large-scale white population withdrawal accompanied by rapid expansion of all black residential areas. This pattern was expected to continue, although perhaps more slowly, since the black immigration from southern areas has declined. It was once estimated that by 1985 the black population in central cities would reach close to 20.8 million—a dramatic increase since the mid-1960s.[10] Not only has the black population of inner cities grown over time, but there is the additional dimension of poverty to be considered. In 1964 almost 30 percent of those living in cities were poor.[11] There has been little reason, until most recently, to believe that this percentage was likely to decrease. Even with the advent of private urban renewal, it is unlikely that entire cities will be restored. However, the process is bringing about dramatic changes in selected sections of inner cities. The process of private urban renewal in the city of Washington, D.C. offers an excellent opportunity to examine the dynamics of these changes in depth. In addition, it is quite likely that the process of private urban renewal in the District is prototypical of the same process in many other cities of the country.

Three areas of the District have been singled out for analysis. These areas are Georgetown, Capitol Hill, and Adams-Morgan. They have been isolated as representative of different phases of the same process. Georgetown represents the first private urban renewal area in the District; Capitol Hill represents an area in rapid transition; Adams-Morgan portrays the initiation of the process. Thus, a historical study following through to contemporary events is presented as a backdrop for developing a model with which to predict areas that are potential private urban renewal targets. This detailed analysis helps answer the following questions:

1. To what extent does the process of private urban renewal involve a change in the population composition of the areas under examination?

2. To what extent does the process involve changes in residential patterns, residential land values, and housing conditions?

3. How is the process of private urban renewal initiated and continued? Specifically, what role do realtors, speculators, formal neighborhood organizations, various governmental agencies, and officials play in the process?

4. What variables can be examined to aid in anticipating residential change before population change begins?

5. In a more general sense, how can knowledge concerning the private urban renewal process in the District be utilized to develop a predictive model for other cities?

The chapters in this book have been arranged with the foregoing questions in mind. Chapter 2 is a discussion and critique of urban ecological theory. It includes a discussion of the literature on residential segregation and reverse blockbusting, because these two phenomena are frequently raised in connection with the private urban renewal process. The third chapter offers a historical portrait of the District from its inception to the beginning of the private urban renewal process. This is offered to familiarize readers with the District and to provide a background for the process in the specific areas of investigation. Chapter 4 is an analysis of the three private urban renewal areas specified as well as of citywide changes from 1940 to the present. Demographic characteristics of the populations involved and changes in residential land use and property value are examined. Much of the analysis is based on census data available to 1970, although it is supplemented by more recent data where available and by interviews with principals involved in the process. While there may be some question about relying on 1970 data, they are indicative of the trend being examined. Additionally, it is unreasonable both from an intellectual perspective and from a policy perspective to wait until perhaps 1982 or 1983 to examine a process that is well underway, particularly one that may have long-range consequences for the cities in which it is occurring. The fifth chapter is a discussion of the role of zoning and historical preservation in regard to private urban renewal. It offers an analysis of local community involvement in attempts to gain control over zoning. Chapter 6 is a discussion of the social and political consequences of private urban renewal. Moreover, it contains an analysis of the conflicts being generated by this process and a discussion of the issue of social class and race in relation to residential housing patterns. The last chapter is a summary of information describing the private urban renewal process both nationally and locally. It contains an analysis of the various components of the process. This chapter posits a two-variable model for use in identifying area change. It further describes the phases of the process and presents a model outlining the necessary elements for a successful private urban renewal effort. Moreover, it presents a discussion of the national, regional, and local considerations accounting for the advent of the private urban renewal of inner city neighborhoods.

Notes

1. U.S. Congress, House, Housing Act of 1954, 83rd Cong., 1954, H.R. 590.

2. U.S. Congress, House, Housing Act of 1958, 85th Cong., 1958, H.R. 1091.

3. See, for example, Hugh Mields, Jr., *Federally Assisted New Communities: New Dimensions in Urban Development* (Washington, D.C.: Urban Land Institute, 1973).

4. See, for example, Herbert J. Gans, *The Urban Villagers* (New York: Free Press, 1962).

5. See, for example: Reynolds Farley, "Suburban Persistence," *American Sociological Review* 29 (February 1964): 38-47; Hal H. Winsborough, "An Ecological Approach to the Theory of Suburbanization," *American Journal of Sociology* 68 (March 1963): 565-570.

6. See, for example: Thomas F. Pettigrew, "Attitudes on Race and Housing: A Social Psychological View," in *Segregation in Residential Areas*, ed. Amos H. Hawley and Vincent P. Rock (Washington, D.C.: National Academy of Sciences, 1973); H.V. Savitch, "Black Cities/White Suburbs: Domestic Colonialism As an Interpretive Idea," *Annals of the American Academy of Political and Social Science* (September 1978), pp. 118-134.

7. *Displacement: City Neighborhoods in Transition* (Washington, D.C.: National Urban Coalition, 1978).

8. *Neighborhood Diversity, Hearings before the Committee on Banking, Housing and Urban Affairs*, U.S. Senate, 95th Cong., 2nd Sess., July 7 and 8, 1977.

9. "Back-to-the-City: a national look at making neighborhood preservation successful," Conference papers, St. Paul, Minnesota, September 26-29, 1975; *Preservation News* 15 (July 1975): 1-11; Thomas J. Black, *Private-Market Housing Renovation in Central Cities: An Urban Land Institute Survey* (Washington, D.C.: Urban Land Institute, 1975).

10. Report of the National Advisory Commission on Civil Disorders, *The Future of Cities* (Washington, D.C.: Government Printing Office, 1969), p. 449.

11. Report of the National Commission on Urban Problems, *Building the American City* (Washington, D.C.: Government Printing Office, 1968), p. 109.

2 Theoretical Considerations and Urban History

A major difficulty encountered in any study of urban social change is the lack of an appropriate theoretical perspective. This is, in fact, true of the study of social change on a general level. An inability to perceive change until it is considerably underway is part of the difficulty. For example, sociologists did not predict the urban riots of the 1960s, nor did they anticipate the coming of the Black Power movement, the student movement, and/or the antiwar movement. It is true that there exist a number of very acceptable *a factori* analyses of these phenomena, but the difficulty of identifying potential change at its inception remains a handicap.

Urban areas have been a focal point for study since at least the turn of the century, and hundreds of empirical studies have been conducted. While there is a great deal of available literature specific to particular cities and particular problems, there is little agreement within the discipline regarding terminology, area of emphasis, or particular models for use in urban analysis. This observation is not unique. In 1938, Louis Wirth stated: "In the rich literature on the city we look in vain for a theory of urbanism presenting in a systematic fashion the available knowledge concerning the city as a social entity. . . ."[1]

Nearly twenty years ago Gideon Sjoberg stated that sociology has no general theory of urbanism, only theoretical orientations.[2] What he perceives to be lacking is an integrated theory about American cities. Ten years ago Anselm Strauss made a similar assertion, arguing that we have yet to develop a useful urban theory.[3] Benjamin Chinitz suggests that: "The natural inclination of a scientist when confronted with a new problem is to try to solve it with old tools. When he is finally convinced that the old tools will not do the job, he retreats to his shop to fashion some new tools."[4]

In the field of urban sociology this type of retreat has yet to occur. There are, however, a series of paradigms that have been used for urban analyses. While it may not be possible to present an integrated theoretical perspective that would allow for describing as well as predicting the future course of urban events, it is possible to utilize available information and to rework these paradigms by adding some new dimensions to already existing knowledge. In this manner we can explain how we arrived at the existent urban scene and can, perhaps, anticipate where we may be going.

Urban Ecological Theory

The urban ecological model has often been used in studies of population change. (There are other paradigms for use in urban analysis; however, they are of little value in discussing urban social change.) To date, it is the model most frequently used to describe residential mobility in urban areas. It is one of the first models to have been developed, originating at the University of Chicago in the late 1920s. In addition to use in population change and mobility studies, this model has been used to examine particular behavior and specific problems within urban environments.[5] A major concern of early urban ecologists was the discovery of principles explaining how human populations adapted to the natural environment and how social groups and institutions developed specific territorial arrangements, particularly in urban areas. Ecological distribution is interpreted as the spatial distribution of individuals grounded in a conscious pattern of physical relationships. Thus, it is no accident that spatial arrangements result in the patterns they ultimately manifest.

To a large extent the ecological model is an analogous one. In their attempt to develop a science of the city, most early analysts approached the study of the human community from a standpoint similar to that of plant ecologists addressing the study of the plant community. The analogy is one wherein the dynamics of urban development are perceived to follow much the same processes as those in the world of flora and fauna. The world of plants requires territory in which to settle and to seek roots, water, and procreative potential. The assumption made by urban ecologists is that people too attach themselves to areas, and their lives and livelihoods become dependent on this particular space.

This attachment to space is characterized as the natural area.[6] Natural areas do not develop by chance or random event, but as a result of homogeneous land use. An outstanding example of the urban ecological model outlining natural areas is the concentric circle pattern developed by Ernest W. Burgess.[7] As originally conceived, the concentric circle pattern is an ideal type—one that is assumed to be universally observable in all kinds of urban communities. According to Burgess, cities grow from the core out, in much the same manner as an apple. Surrounding the core is a series of concentric circles. The characteristic spatial pattern of these concentric circles is: (1) a central core which is the business center; (2) an area of residential deterioration which is often called the "zone in transition", (3) an area of workingmen's homes; (4) an area of better residences; and (5) the commuters' zones.[8] The growth and development of these zones is portrayed not as a random accident but rather as a pattern that results as the specific forces of competition generated in the dominant area operate.

Oscar Handlin's description of the formation of urban ghettos in the United States illustrates these forces in operation.[9] What occurs is that the immigrants arrive with little money and few resources and thus have limited choice in the selection of living space. They occupy residential areas that are no longer desired by the original occupants. Part of the reason why these residential areas are no longer desirable is that they are being encroached upon by the expanding business center. They are becoming dirty, congested, and noisy, and the well-to-do are unwilling to live in close proximity to these conditions. However, this same expansion that makes an area undesirable for residential purposes creates a high real estate value for the property. Ultimately, residential buildings in these areas will be torn down. The land will be sold for commercial expansion, and new office buildings and factories will be built. In the interim it is not profitable to spend money on the upkeep of the existing structures and thus they are allowed to deteriorate. But, these structures do become homes for those with limited housing choices. Large old residential buildings that had once housed the relatively affluent are subdivided and rented to immigrants. There is little loss of revenue in terms of upkeep on the buildings, and the rent collected provides adequate profit until the buildings are sold for demolition. Handlin's work typifies the urban ecological explanation of the process of competition, wherein the central business district, the dominant area, must expand. As this expansion takes place, the dominant area begins competition with the zone immediately outside it—the zone in transition. As a result of this competition, land values in the transitional zone are forced up, but the buildings and the neighborhoods deteriorate. Residents able to afford higher rents and the cost of commuting begin to move to the periphery. The same process was described by Homer Hoyt in 1939, and this perspective dominates the direction urban ecological studies have taken. According to Hoyt: "High rent or high-grade residential neighborhoods must almost necessarily move outward toward the periphery of the city. The wealthy seldom reverse their steps and move backward into the obsolete houses which they are giving up."[10]

Each zone extends its area by the invasion of the next outer zone. Thus urban areas change as their uses change in the struggle for urban space.

When the change from residential to business land use is complete, the process of ecological succession is halted until the cycle begins again. While ecological theory recognizes that populations are involved in this process, they are not considered to be prime movers, but rather, subject to the forces of dominance and competition. Over time the original notion of discrete zones has been replaced by the notion of gradients. But implicit in the model is the idea that the population distribution becomes increasingly homogeneous and distinct as cities grow in size.[11] The ultimate portrait of an urban population describes this distribution: "Blue collar workers, individuals without spouses, Blacks and ethnic groups would live most frequently in the central parts of the city; white collar workers, married couples with children, white and native Americans would be found most often on the outskirts."[12]

In addition to the forces of competition and dominance, there are two

other major principles in urban ecological theory. These latter are represented
by the invasion-succession cycle. Most of the early urban sociological literature
concerning population change employs these terms. Invasion describes the
replacement of majority group members by a minority group, with these terms
being used to describe the resulting aggregate changes. The invading group is
usually lower on the social and ethnic scale than the original residents, although
this is not always the case. As early as 1925, ecological theorists hypothesized
that the invasion-succession pattern could go in either direction; that is, an
upper-income group could invade as well as a lower-income group.[13] However,
available literature indicates that most studies, with the exception of Walter
Firey's work on Boston, have tended to focus on invasion of the latter; this is
one of the few sociological studies wherein the invading group is of higher
status than the original residents. Firey's work will be discussed in a later section, since it is a modification of urban ecological theory. The dominant theoretical focus, however, has been on invasion-succession as characterized by groups
of low social status invading areas populated by groups of higher status. The
probable reason for this concentration is that when the urban ecological school
first developed, enormous waves of immigrants were arriving in the United
States: "Between 1840 and 1870, the population of New York City mounted
by fully 50 percent every ten years; for every two people at the start of the
decade, there were three at its end . . . struggling for the space formerly occupied
by one . . .[14]

Poor Europeans continued to immigrate to American cities until 1924,
when Congress adopted the National Origins quota system.[15] Since this phenomenon was of major concern to the developing school of urban ecology,
the struggle for space among the rapidly growing American population was a
major influence in the development of the concepts of competition and dominance.

As stated earlier, the urban ecological model is an analagous one. In the
study of plant ecology it has been determined that plant communities are
displaced by plants of other species over time. Such factors as soil, climate, and
the peculiarities of the species are involved in the change. In the human community social organization undergoes a similar change when groups of different
economic and cultural levels displace each other. Moreover, while most of this
literature has concentrated on run-down or slumlike areas, because the direction
of the model is an outward expansion of circles with lower-status groups moving
into areas where those of higher social status are succeeding, it is important to
note that in early urban ecological theory, lower-status groups invaded only
areas that were already on the way to being abandoned by another group of
higher status. The implication is that lower-status groups can only move up
when an area is already beginning to deteriorate. The slum dweller is not the
creator but merely the inheritor of the slum. Konrad Bercovici's description of

the growth of Negro Harlem is characteristic of the invasion-succession aspects of ecological theory.

Bercovici begins his analysis with the history of the black migration from the Southern United States. He describes Harlem as an area already experiencing a real estate slump. The local resident population of Harlem was in the process of moving to better housing, leaving behind the old-fashioned buildings of Harlem. As a result, there were empty apartments in every building. Apparently one landlord set off the mass white exodus by renting an apartment to a mulatto family: "The white population fled as if in dread of a contagious disease. Block after block was deserted by whites . . ."[16]

Two important points emerge in Bercovici's analysis. First, he stresses that the area was already on its way to being abandoned by white tenants before any blacks moved into the area. Second, the dimension of race appears as a strong factor accelerating white outmigration from the area.

Inclusion of the variable of race is an important dimension, because most classical urban ecological analyses are not concerned with the status of the population as a primary emphasis. Rather, racial/ethnic description of populations is generally provided only for background purposes. Like its parent science plant ecology, urban ecology ignores social factors. The process of change is described in nonsocial terms, and the dynamics involved are the ecological complex composed of the population, social organization, environment, and technology, all of which are defined as external physical conditions. Amos Hawley suggests that, "Organization is a property of a population and not of an aggregate of individuals."[17] The moving force behind the urban ecological model is competition for scarce resources in an open-market situation. What occurs is that all interests of a social nature become subsumed in the interest of minimizing cost. For example, Robert McKenzie states, "Underlying all forms of urban segregation are the factors of income and rent."[18] This perspective is further illustrated in the work of Noel Gist and L.A. Halbert in their examination of Chicago: "There is a tendency for urbanites to select a residential land area for which their income is adequate . . . . Undoubtedly, many immigrants are forced by economic necessity to live with other immigrants although their inclinations are to move elsewhere."[19]

This approach, emphasizing income, cost, and scarcity of resources has been characterized by Sidney Willheld as the materialistic view of urban ecology.[20] That is, urban ecological theory in its most classical form can be summarily defined as the study of the relationship between a human population and its environment. Theoretical emphasis is placed on the external physical conditions superimposed on a population; analyses are devoid of consideration of values, motives, and interests on the part of the population, these being considered merely psychological phenomena. An illustration of this theory in application is manifest in Louis Wirth's study of Jews in the United States. In his discussion of the ghettolike living arrangements within which they find themselves, he says: ". . . Each area in the city is suited for some one function better than for any other . . . Each seeks his own habitat much like the plants and animals in the world of nature . . ."[21]

Modifications and Urban Ecological Theory

The concentric zone theory was received with some criticism, primarily because of its rigidity. The earliest arguments with this model took the form of offering supplementary models with which to expand the original premises of the theory. The concepts underlying the theory were not challenged; rather, variations on the same model were put forth. The most outstanding amendment to the original theory was made by Homer Hoyt, who devised sector theory. According to sector theory, any particular land use tends to grow out from the center along a given axis, forming a sector. The same land use would then exist from the center of the periphery.[22] This model is not substantially different from the original concentric rings, since the basic premises of the original urban ecological model are accepted as valid. The same type of determinism operates in accordance with the concepts of invasion, succession, competition, and dominance. Around 1940, the model was amended again to include the multiple nuclei theory. In this model there are a number of central cores, all of which have rings moving out from them. However, once again the basic premises of the model remain unchallenged.

It is theoretically possible for the invasion-succession cycle to move in either direction. That is, it is possible for a high-income population to reverse its steps and return to the city. However, apart from Walter Firey's study of Boston, this dimension of the model has been empirically neglected. Firey offers the first moderate departure from the urban ecological approach in *Land Use in Central Boston.*[23] First he argues that social values must be taken into account when examining land utilization. Second, his study is one of the few in which the process of invasion-succession does not follow the dominant trend. He demonstrates a reverse procedure in Boston, wherein land on Commonwealth Avenue is purchased by a group of socially prominent people. This in turn sets off a wave of buying in the area, converting what was becoming a slum into an elegant area. It is difficult to isolate the factors involved in this reverse process, but it is the social prestige of the original group that encourages the inmigration of others. What motivates the original prestigious population is what Firey calls "fetishism." This is a process whereby the symbolic attributes of a spatial area become end-values in themselves. The "persistence of reputation" or group fondness for a physical area produces a solidarity among some people (in this case a wealthy group) that overrides knowledge that the area is deteriorating. This phenomenon motivates the group to reclaim the area rather than to move out to the periphery in the pattern predicted by previous urban ecological theorists.

An important consideration in this particular study is Firey's growing disenchantment with a model that he perceives as sterile because of its failure to consider the factor of human motivation. However, it must be borne in mind that Firey is not rejecting the original premises made by the urban ecologists: rather he is attempting to add a necessary dimension that he argues is missing from the original model.

Urban Ecological Theory: A Critique

There are myriad shortcomings in the urban ecological model, most of which are familiar to students of the urban environment. Perhaps the most basic problem of the model is that it originates in an American school, having roots in no other body of literature. As such, it is ahistorical. The dimensions of time, history, past trend, and personal preference have little room in the model. This has been noted by other critics as well.[24] It would seem obvious that different histories would dictate different developmental patterns. However, because the model is ahistorical, there is an assumption that urban dynamics are universally uniform. In fact, although Burgess points out that some cities do depart from the premises of the model, these variations are viewed as "interesting minor modifications."[25]

Generally, the model is predicated on a deterministic premise. Things must go into their proper places. Yet nowhere in the literature is there described a modus operandi by which these phenomena find their proper places in space. The model is deterministic, but it lacks a dimension explaining why certain patterns must occur.

Another obvious flaw in this model is its inapplicability to the new cities in the United States. Los Angeles is an example of a city where one would be hard-pressed to identify a central core, much less concentric rings. There is some question as to whether it could be superimposed on Southern cities at all. In fact, a review of the spatial composition of U.S. cities leads to the conclusion that the model is not useful except perhaps for describing the development of large industrial cities.

Another difficulty with this model is its assumption of open market competition for space and of spontaneous competition. It is important to note that the nature of competition is not the same as that of conflict. On the one hand, when a neighborhood or a residential community is exploited overtly for economic gain and when panic among the residents is generated consciously, conflict is created.

Competition, on the other hand, as perceived by urban ecologists, is essentially an unconscious process, because the city is perceived in terms of physical growth, devoid of human motivation and/or desire. As a result, urban ecologists viewed populations as actors in an already set production. Growth occurs in stages. The stages are predetermined. Ultimately everything arrives at its proper place. Again, the analogy of the plant world is most appropriate. Just as annuals can be crowded out by weeds, one human population is displaced by another. But, there is no intent, consciousness of progression, or conflict involved in the process.

All the literature concerning the phenomenon of blockbusting belies this theory. When blacks entered the marketplace in search of housing, the premises collapsed. Blacks were greeted with hostility, threats, and violence. The congregating of blacks in segregated residential areas is not accidental. Rather it is a result of conscious restrictive covenants, both de facto and de jure. Once this became the case, the ecological model, built on the premises of an open market situation and spontaneous competition for scarce resources, could no longer be applied. Spontaneity is a built-in component of the ecological model, but there is much evidence to suggest that planning, organization, and concerted investment of time and energy on the part of realtors is the moving force behind much residential segregation. Realtors are not the only actors. There is evidence that zoning regulations have been utilized to enforce residential segregation. As a result there are some serious contradictions between ecological theory and what others perceive as reality. That is, ecological theory does not take into account human motivations, values, ideas, or ideologies. Its focus is aggregates. However, studies of residential segregation suggest that many actors are involved in either maintaining or establishing certain patterns for certain neighborhoods. The result is that ecological theory ignores or dismisses what active participants engaged in changing residential patterns perceive as paramount. This is well illustrated by the urban ecological concept of organization. A quotation from a work by Frederick Engels is much in keeping with some descriptions of urban analysts commenting on the American scene. Engels states:

> ... the brutal indifference, the unfeeling isolation of each in his private interest becomes the more repellant and offensive, the more these individuals are crowded together within a limited space ... The dissolution of mankind into nomads of which each one has a separate principle, the world of atoms, is here carried out to its utmost extreme ... Hence it comes too, that the social war, the war of each against all, is here openly declared ... Everywhere barbarous indifference, hard egotism on one hand, and nameless misery on the other, everywhere social warfare, everyman's house in a state of seige ...[26]

If this was put into more modified language, it could as easily have been written by any number of urban ecologists describing the zone of transition within the concentric circles. The difference is emphasis. Engels argues that the growth of London's slums and the maintenance of a poor population is inherent to capitalism. The urban ecological theorists also describe the dynamics of urban areas in economic terms. But the latter emphasis is in keeping with the system of free enterprise. Market considerations are significant in urban ecological analyses. Again, the components of the model are population, environment, technology, and organization. Economic considerations are subsumed under the category of organization.

However, it is assumed that an uncontrolled, free, competitive system exists. Within urban ecological theory there is no recognition of the possibility that an economic system can be deliberately manipulated to provide profit for some while permanently depriving others. The assumption is that all are free to compete under equal circumstances. Urban ecological theory operates on the assumption that ultimately all incomes can rise and all living standards can improve. It assumes that after a period of struggle, everyone moves "up and out," making way for the next wave of poor, who will then face the same challenges.

The ecological paradigm does not acknowledge the possibility of permanent poverty, nor does it acknowledge racism, manipulation, and coercion as factors in residential patterns. It cannot acknowledge that slum areas are an ongoing source of profit for some and a permanent source of deprivation for others. It is possible that one reason for the persistent use of the model is that it is compatible with the general premises of the society wherein it was developed; its description of population mobility is in keeping with the "American dream."

Another difficulty with the ecological model is that it is unidirectional. It hypothesizes a constant development of rings expanding outward from the central core. According to this model the outer ring of Washington should ultimately merge with the outer ring of Baltimore.[27] While it is true that there has been enormous suburban growth over the last two decades, much of this growth has resulted in relatively self-contained entities that are neither part of nor dependent on the central city for many of the services that they receive and provide. We do speak of the growth of megalopoli when describing the expansion of population from Boston to Atlanta, but there are still great expanses of rural area between Standard Metropolitan Statistical Areas. Additionally, these areas are unlikely to fill in as anticipated by urban ecological theorists simply because they are not necessarily connected to the inner city.

There are other important criticisms of ecological theory in the literature. One of the more comprehensive critiques is offered by Sylvia Fava, who argues that all four of the major elements in ecological analysis—population, environment, technology, and organization—have changed.[28] This obviously is an accurate statement. Americans have become increasingly mobile over time. As a result, ethnic areas have been dispersed and replaced by residential patterns based on social class similarities. Populations are considerably larger and more heterogeneous, particularly since, with the exception of racial considerations, most restrictive covenants in housing have broken down. In ecological analyses it is necessary to isolate homogeneous areas when attempting to apply the

theory empirically. Given the geographical mobility of Americans and the suburban expansion, it is difficult to isolate homogeneous urban centers, apart
from those housing black populations. Even black populations are not essentially
homogeneous, since blacks tend to live in ghettos regardless of socioeconomic
status. Furthermore, changes in technology could not have been anticipated
by the early ecological theorists. In a very short time technological changes have
occurred that are so dramatic that they constitute a change of order rather than
of degree. For example, in the 1930s the automobile was a relatively scarce item.
Today almost every family owns at least one automobile. Rapid transit is com-
monplace, and public transportation systems have grown rapidly. As a result,
the environment has changed dramatically, and communities are no longer
either autonomous or self-sufficient. Probably the most significant change is in
the nature of social organization. The free market situation and the autonomy
of local communities taken for granted by ecological theorists no longer exist,
if in fact they ever existed. One example of dramatic change is illustrated by
decentralization within these areas. Thus we have town, county, city, state, and
federal governments interacting; as a result, places of residence, of taxation, of
shopping, of recreation, and of school have become separated jurisdictionally
over time. There is little uniformity within metropolitan areas. Not all areas
receive the same types of urban services, nor do they need to utilize the same
types of facilities. The result is a separation of services, needs, administration,
and finance. Planning is often a central function. Areas do not make their own
decisions but are part of central planning agencies affected by decisions made
on a variety of governmental levels.

Residential Segregation

There is a large body of theoretical material describing residential segregation.
One of these descriptions is offered by Herbert Blumer who, like Park and
Burgess before him, views the formation of diversified areas of residence as a
natural and spontaneous process. He expands the theory somewhat by stating
that ecological differentiation is affected by three forces: (1) neutral—level of
income and accessibility to work; (2) attraction—the wish to live among people
with whom one identifies oneself; and (3) rejection—the wish to avoid people
one views as unacceptable.[29]

Alvin Schorr offers another explanation of residential segregation. His
argument is that there are a number of forces guaranteeing that different types
of groups do not mix and that we are sorted into neighborhoods of specified
income, specified color, specified religion, or a specified combination of all
these. He writes:

The forces that produce residential segregation are familiar. They are
as follows: (1) the family cycle where people with children migrate to

the suburbs; (2) Racial segregation where a city council or housing authority locate low-cost dwellings in renewal areas or yield to opposition in higher cost areas; (3) Local and state tax structures where officials will increase property taxes to provide services for some and avoid tax increases by zoning actions to prevent developments that would make increases necessary; (4) Banks, builders, and real estate brokers combine to insure pure poverty of one neighborhood and pure wealth of another. A myth has been constructed from these forces mentioned. The myth is simple: If someone with less money or who is inferior moves next door, then one is not safe in his bed, one's children are not safe in school and one's mortgage is endangered.[30]

In 1910, only one Negro in four lived in an urban place; by 1950, two-thirds of the nation's Negroes lived in urban places and 9.7 percent of the urban population was Negro. In 1970, over one-third of all Negroes in the United States lived in the Northeast, where they made up one-tenth of the population.[31] An immediate problem occurring as a result of this inmigration emerged around housing. The immigrating blacks, like the immigrant groups that preceded them, tended to move into the least desirable areas. As their numbers increased, they began expansion into other areas. Unlike other immigrant groups, blacks were not accepted in residential areas. Initially agreements to keep them out of residential areas were tacit, but at the end of World War II residential tensions began to produce more violent exchanges. For example, Governor Adlai Stevenson was forced to declare martial law in Cicero, Illinois because of racial violence in 1951. In 1952, a mob of Chicago citizens attempted to burn down a two-family house after hearing rumors that Negros were planning to move into the building.[32] None of these things had happened to other immigrant groups regardless of national origins and despite their poverty.

In attempting to comprehend the difficulties of residential segregation, most empirical investigations have focused on the relationship between black inmigration or invasion and the effect of property prices in the areas. The reason for this type of investigation is that most Americans articulate their reasons for leaving areas under invasion in terms of their fear that the value of their property will be reduced. The results of most studies of the relationship between black invasion and price drop do not justify their fears. Reporting on a study of price changes in two Chicago areas, Charles Benson concludes that when an area is originally threatened by transition prices drop. But once the transition is completed prices are again controlled by supply and demand. Regardless of the racial composition of an area, prices ultimately rise again and are in keeping with citywide costs.[33] Robert Weaver's findings are similar to those offered by Benson. He concludes: ". . . that much depends upon the state of the total housing market and manner in which colored people enter an area . . . *There is no one universal effect of Negro occupancy* upon property values."[34]

Two things come to mind when reviewing this particular body of literature. First, while there has been some study of property values as neighborhoods are invaded by blacks, there has been little study of the process underlying changes in property values and little examination of the *role* of various actors in bringing about these changes. Second, despite expanded Civil Rights legislation and Fair Housing Acts, there does not appear to be much change in the traditional pattern of residential segregation that characterizes most of America.[35]

The majority of empirical studies indicate that regardless of either legislation or intent, there are few cases where integration has been maintained in a residential setting.[36] Empirical investigations indicate that the belief that housing values will fall upon integration is erroneous. As a result, accounting for the mass exodus that takes place when invasion begins is difficult. John McDermott and Dennis Clark suggest that an irrational process operates wherein people cease to think logically and become victimized by beliefs in myths and stereotypes.[37] When this occurs they no longer know exactly what they believe but act on the basis of common rumors that suggest that the neighborhood is "going" and that they "should get out while it is still possible."

Blockbusting

One phenomenon that has been investigated in connection with white exodus, and one that is being raised again in relation to private urban renewal, is blockbusting. This practice is considered "unethical" because of the professional ethics of the realtor and the policy position to which he adheres.[38] The Fair Housing Act of 1968 contains a legal definition of blockbusting. It is described as a practice: "For a profit, to induce or attempt to induce any person to sell or rent any dwelling by representations regarding the entry into the neighborhood of a person or persons of a particular race, color, religion, or national origin."[39]

There is little debate about the fact that racial residential segregation is the norm among housing patterns in the United States. Regardless of socioeconomic levels, blacks live in ghettos. Ghetto, in this context, is not to be taken as synonymous with slum—the more frequently used contemporary connotation. Given the prejudice expressed by white Americans against blacks, it is quite possible that ghettos are self-selected communities wherein people feel secure regardless of what they otherwise could afford economically.[40] Moreover, in the District of Columbia as well as in many other U.S. cities, there are extremely expensive black residential areas. However, housing segregation in general is increasing, and it has been predicted that the United States is moving toward apartheid if the cycle of increasing black cities encircled by white suburbs is not halted.[41]

There have been some studies predicting that a few Negro families in an area may not result in white succession.[42] The question then arises as to what "a few Negro families" means and how "a few" are perceived. Some studies suggest that there is a "tipping point," in terms of Negro visibility, which sets off a wave of succession.[43] Exactly what constitutes a tipping point is not clear. Some writers have suggested that it is reached when the majority of an urban voting population is black.[44] There are some studies suggesting that the tipping point, or the offsetting of the tenuous residential racial balance, has been accelerated by blockbusting. Blockbusting is very simple: a realtor or a group of real estate agents descend on an area. Preferably the area is already somewhat mixed, but this is not absolutely necessary. Obviously there must be enough of a black population in the vicinity to make the threat real. These realtors then suggest to white residents that the area is becoming black. "If you don't sell now, you may wind up being the last white on the block" is the usual message. Predictably, panic follows, setting off a wave of white succession from the area. Simultaneously, the black population of the area increases. A detailed account of this process is offered by Jack Rothman, based on his study of population change in Queens, New York:

> Racially changing neighborhoods have in recent years reached widespread and troubling proportions. Almost every city dweller can call to mind some neighborhood that was transformed almost overnight from a solidly white to what became a solidly Negro district . . . One of the chief causes of rapid neighborhood change (and consequently of residential segregation) is the presence of prejudice in so many of our white citizens . . . But this prejudice constitutes only the most obvious starting point in attempting to understand the dynamics of the change pattern. What is less known is that in addition to this "spontaneous" process, there are purposeful, efficiently organized "unspontaneous" influences at work—the Ghetto Makers who consciously trigger off these personal predispositions and channel them into large-scale movements. These Ghetto Makers play at least as large a part in fostering segregation as do public attitudes, and their role needs to be laid bare and understood if we are ever to make headway in coping with the problem . . . Standing at their head are a core of unethical or prejudiced real estate brokers.[45]

In a Chicago study it was reported that there are very specific patterns in the way in which real estate brokers work in certain residential zones. The policy they tacitly operate under is called "exclusion." Exclusion is based on the belief that once an area and the property contained within it are transferred from white to black groups, it is lost to the white group forever. As a result, brokers are selective as to which areas they are willing to show to black clients unless the area is peripheral to an area that has already been invaded by blacks. In that case, brokers are frequently active in blockbusting, which opens up the peripheral area to blacks. The justification for this conduct is the brokers' belief that it is necessary to take social meaning into account when doing business, and that the traditions, customs, beliefs, and aspirations of the general social milieu must be considered. Most of the brokers interviewed in this study indicated that they would not introduce blacks into an area where they had friends who owned property. They would certainly not introduce them into an area where they lived.[46] The tendency appears to be one wherein people are directed toward neighborhoods that are deemed suitable for them, whether or not these neighborhoods are their particular choice. This process has been documented in selected areas across the coutnry, but there is not much literature available that is comprehensive.

Theoretical Inadequacies: District of Columbia—
A Case in Point

With regard to the development of the District of Columbia, it is difficult to imagine the applicability of urban ecological theory. First, there has never been a central business district from which rings or concentric circles could develop to a periphery. The only semblance of a central business zone existed in Georgetown, which was not initially part of the District. Second, the District is one of the least industrial cities in the United States. Third, while there was some European immigration into the District, the numbers were limited. Moreover, this population did not move into housing that was being abandoned by the more affluent. Rather, the immigrants moved into working-class areas that did not deteriorate until the black migration waves began, post-World War II.

Residential housing patterns in the District do not approximate those predicted by an ecological model. From its founding, there has been a substantial black population in the District. Until approximately 1930 residential housing patterns, like those in many Southern cities, were integrated, although *integrated* may not be the proper term to describe these housing patterns. It is perhaps more appropriate to say that blacks and whites lived within close proximity. In fact, in 1897, when the District experienced a severe housing shortage as a result of a large black immigration, whites did not flee the area. Instead lots were divided, and rear portions were sold separately. This resulted in the black population living in the alleys of white residential areas.[47]

According to Constance McLaughlin Green, this housing pattern grew out of the customary living arrangements of the South, wherein slaves usually lived in the rear lot quarters of their master's property.[48] For the most part the early black population of the District was engaged in domestic work. It was thus quite natural for them to live in close proximity to whites. In addition, despite various black codes, in the District this population was allowed to purchase property, and frequently did so, in areas where whites resided. This pattern was maintained until as late as the turn of the century. In the early part of the century almost every city in the Northeast that housed a sizeable black population was showing indications of residential segregation. In 1909 and 1919, surveys show blacks paying 25 to 50 percent more rent than whites for the same type of accommodations in every big city except Washington.[49]

Discrimination in housing in the District began as late as 1930, probably due to the advent of a large influx of poor Southern blacks. Additional pressure was brought to the situation by the severe housing shortage that occurred in the District during this period. The real changes in residential housing patterns began in the 1950s. Once the black population began to outnumber the white, the typical blockbusting pattern emerged. Employing the usual tactics of implying that property values would plunge if a black family moved into an area, "speculators bought up whole residential blocks cheap, sold the houses to Negroes at inflated prices, and then repeated the process in another block.[50] This account typifies the process by which residential segregation is created. There is no room for this explanation within the premises of ecological theory.

Private Urban Renewal: An Anomaly in Residential Housing Patterns?

It is unnecessary to dwell at length on the contemporary urban scene, because there is little debate about the assessment that for the past twenty-five years U.S. cities have been moving steadily toward crisis. The problems appear to be endless, and their resolution has been elusive. The quality of urban climates has continued to deteriorate, despite enormous expenditures and efforts to repair the damage or at least to stem the tide of further decline. It is relatively easy to comprehend this lack of solutions by recognizing that the problems encompass such ills as poor education, high crime rates, high unemployment rates, poverty, inadequate housing, pollution, racism, and financial collapse. As of 1970, it still appeared that population growth in central cities would be predominantly nonwhite and that approximately fifteen major cities would have black majority populations by 1985.[51] Without attempting to discuss why the decline has taken place, it is certainly fair to state that, since at least 1955, the cities of the United States have been in decline.

Something new, however, is underway in residential housing patterns. Since 1976, at least sixty newspaper articles, ten magazine articles, and several surveys have discussed the process of private urban renewal (PUR). These include descriptions from such diverse cities as New Orleans, Louisiana; Richmond, Virginia; Lowell, Massachusetts; and Baltimore, Maryland; to cite a few.

A recent survey released by the National Urban Coalition begins by stating that: ". . . the emergence of a new breed of relatively welloff "urban pioneers" and developers—has created an uneven but definite in-migration of middle class homeowners and renters who are taking up residence in city neighborhoods that they and financial institutions once shunned.[52]

This survey offers an examination of forty-four U.S. cities, all of which have populations of a million or more, all of which indicate some degree of private urban renewal (PUR) in progress.

Illustrative of these cities is Alexandria, Virginia. Old Town, Alexandria is a small section of a city. It is composed almost exclusively of houses dating to the Colonial period. Once a run-down area, it has been privately renewed over time and is currently an elegant section of the city of Alexandria. Over the past few years Old Town has been expanding into the less historical sections of the city. The expansion of the PUR area has inflated the prices of housing in the area adjoining Old Town. It has set off a wave of selling wherein the renter population is being displaced by persons interested in purchasing housing for restoration.

In an Advisory Referendum held by persons who own homes in the adjoining section of the city, it was proposed that a plan be put into effect that would artifically depress the prices of houses in that area and preserve the neighborhood for lower-income families. If the legislation was approved, the National Endowment for the Arts would finance the conservation of the homes of long-time residents in the area. The proposal recommended that homes in the area be sold through a community cooperative at prices lower than the seller could get on the open market. It was believed that such a plan would stabilize both the population and the housing prices in the area.

The homeowners in the affected community are predominantly black, lower-income families. Some of these people are being moved out of the area because of the process of PUR. Some of the residents are homeowners who are finding it increasingly difficult to resist the offers of speculators. Others are finding it increasingly difficult to pay the rising real estate taxes. Despite these difficulties, the homeowners in this community have rejected the proposed plan by an overwhelming majority.[53]

Another example of PUR is the "Fan" area of Richmond, Virginia. This is an area that partially surrounds the central core of Richmond. The area is characterized by turn-of-the-century houses. Over the past twenty years the area has been transformed from a slum to a neighborhood that is 99.9 percent white, expensive, and desirable. It is beginning now to expand into the area immediately surrounding it. The bulk of the restoration in the Fan took place between 1965 and 1975. The spread into surrounding areas continues.[54]

In Brooklyn, New York the process is occurring in Boerum Hill, Park Slope, Cobble Hill, and Fort Greene. In 1965, Boerum Hill was a run-down area. Its population was primarily Puerto Rican. By 1975, the population had decreased by approximately 6,000 Spanish-speaking people.[55] In New York City the process of PUR is known as "brown-stoning." In spite of its general popularity, "This movement back to the city has been going on slowly under the noses of the city government but the city has done little to help it.[56]

Part of the difficulty in measuring the impact of PUR is that 1970 census data are badly outdated, and metropolitan statistics, which are updated to 1974, do not provide tract and block data on a national basis. Perhaps the best available national data are those obtained by the Urban Land Institute. Their findings indicate that almost 50,000 housing units have been renovated in urban areas between 1967 and 1975.[57] While this may appear to represent a trickle rather than a tide, it is clearly indicative of change. Moreover, it is a change that could not have been anticipated, given the existing models for urban analysis. The lack of a predictive dimension lies within the nature of urban theory. First, it is difficult to anticipate the ability to generate comprehensive theory in isolation. Apart from the few Marxist analyses of the urban milieu, urban sociological theory has not allowed for an evaluation of the political and economic dynamics in the larger society.[58] As such, there is a discontinuity between propositions that are developed on a micro level and a general body of theoretical literature within which to examine these propositions. Urban areas do not exist in a vacuum. The dynamics involving any particular entity are intricately connected to the general social structure within which they reside. Without taking these conditions of structure into consideration, theory developed for the examination of particular problems is likely to be sterile.

Other deficiencies in the development of sociological theory result from the continued use of obsolete paradigms. Urban ecological theory has not been truly applicable since the black migration movement into U.S. cities began. At that time its basic premises ceased to be operable. Yet it still dominates contemporary urban analyses. Reliance on models that are no longer viable hampers the effort to develop a systematic body of urban theory. If we could abandon the paradigms that have developed over time—acknowledging our debt to these models for their past contributions—cease debating their merits, and move on to developing theory that encompasses the total social structure of the society, we might develop a comprehensive urban theory.[59]

Finally, we have to consider the possibility that there is not, nor can there be, any universal theoretical framework for urban analysis. One of the basic assumptions concerning theory construction is that a universal theoretical framework can be created that will ultimately be appropriate for analysis in any locale. One of the premises regarding the construction of social theory is that if enough empirical data are collected and enough small-scale studies are conducted, this information will ultimately cumulate into a theoretical framework. As a result, in the field of urban sociology we have literally thousands of case studies. While these studies are not without value, the basic problem has remained: there has been no universal theory for urban analysis. It is likely that the continued search for such a theory is a fruitless task, because it is unlikely that cities will exhibit similarity beyond the scope of particular phenomenon. For example, if slum clearance projects and the construction of public housing destroys the sense of community for people in Boston, it is likely that it has the same effect in Chicago, New York, Los Angeles, and elsewhere. If it is difficult to racially integrate schools in Boston, it is probably difficult to do so in any city with a sizeable black population and an urban ethnic population living in close proximity. If the characteristics of cities are the same, then it is likely that the problems will be the same. However, complications arise from the fact that cities are not the same. The District of Columbia is not a manufacturing city, yet it houses a majority black population. Detroit is an industrial manufacturing city with the same type of population composition. The problems in the District of Columbia, however, are not the same as the problems in Detroit. The same can be said of the school integration issue. There are cities where the problem has been handled with relative ease; in other cities the problem appears insurmountable. We do not know why this is the case. If school integration has not been a problem, is it perhaps because the white population has withdrawn from the public education system? In the District of Columbia the school population is 97 percent black. Integration has not been a problem; it is not even an issue. There are a few elementary schools that have predominantly white enrollments, but there is not a large enough white student population to attempt to bus for integration. The case in Boston is dramatically different and has been and continues to be problematic. There has been much intense examination of the situation in Boston, but little cross-city comparison examining similar phenomenon in different locales.

Concerning housing, we do not know when and why specific neighborhoods will improve and/or decline. But if there is any validity to the claim that smog is a major factor in the decline of affluent areas of Los Angeles, there is reason to believe that what is problematic and creates change in one city may have little to do with any other city.[60] If this is the case, then it is hardly likely that we can develop a universal urban theory. Perhaps the best we can do now is to examine and compare similar phenomena across cities in the hopes of isolating common patterns that relate to these specific dynamics.

There is ample evidence to suggest that the process of private urban renewal is running counter to anticipated trends in many cities of the United States. Sociological examination of the process is, for the most part, lacking. The process of private urban renewal in the city of Washington, District of Columbia, offers an excellent opportunity to redress this imbalance in the literature. Analysis of this process is necessary as a basis of revising and modifying existing sociological theory concerning urbanism and American urban social structure. This book examines the process of private urban renewal, both historically and contemporarily, in three areas of the District of Columbia. It is an attempt to isolate, identify, and describe the dynamics that this process entails in one city. Moreover, an understanding of the dynamics of this process in one city should aid in identifying and predicting the factors to be anticipated concerning the process in other U.S. cities.

Notes

1. Louis Wirth, "Urbanism as a Way of Life," in *Cities and Society*, ed. Paul K. Hatt and Albert J. Reiss Jr. (New York: Free Press, 1951), p. 50.

2. Gideon Sjoberg, "Comparative Urban Sociology," in *Sociology Today*, ed. Robert K. Merton, Leonard Broom, and Leonard S. Cottrell, Jr. (New York: Basic Books, 1959), p. 339.

3. Anselm L. Strauss, "Strategies for Discovering Urban Theory," in *Social Science and the City: A Survey of Research Methods*, ed. Leo F. Schnore (New York: Frederick A. Praeger, 1968), p. 79.

4. Benjamin Chinitz, "Contrasts and Agglomeration: New York and Pittsburgh," in *Urban Economics*, ed. Ronald E. Grieson (Boston: Little, Brown, 1973), p. 26.

5. See, for example, St. Clair Drake and Horace R. Cayton, *Black Metropolis: A Study of Negro Life in a Northern City*, (New York: Harcourt, Brace, 1945); Frederick M. Thrasher, *The Gang* (Chicago: University of Chicago Press, 1927).

6. For an extensive discussion of the natural area see: Robert E. Park, "Human Ecology," *American Journal of Sociology* 42 (1936): 1-15; Donnell M. Pappenfort, "The Ecological Field and the Metropolitan Community," *American Journal of Sociology* 64 (1959): 380-385.

7. Ernest W. Burgess, "The Growth of a City: An Introduction to a Research Project," in *The City*, ed. Robert E. Park (Chicago: University of Chicago Press, 1925), p. 55.

8. For a detailed description of this model see: ibid., pp. 47-62.

9. Oscar Handlin, *The Uprooted* (New York: Grosset and Dunlop, 1951).

10. Homer Hoyt, *The Structure and Growth of Residential Neighborhoods in American Cities* (New York: Ronald Press, 1939), p. 75.

11. Roland K. Hawkes, "Spatial Patterning of Urban Population Characteristics," *American Journal of Sociology* 78 (March 1973): 1216-1235.

12. Ernest W. Burgess, *The Urban Community* (Chicago: University of Chicago Press, 1925), p. 93.

13. Roderick D. McKenzie, "The Scope of Human Ecology," *American Journal of Sociology* 32 (July 1926): part II.

14. Oscar Handlin, *The Uprooted* (New York: Grosset and Dunlop, 1951), p. 145.

15. Peter I. Rose, *The Subject Is Race* (New York: Oxford University Press, 1968), p. 22.

16. Konrad Bercovici, *Around the World in New York* (New York: Century, 1924), p. 216.

17. Amos H. Hawley "Ecology and Human Ecology," *Social Forces* 12 (May 1944): 401.

18. Robert D. McKenzie, *The Metropolitan Community* (New York: McGraw Hill, 1933), p. 247.

19. Noel P. Gist and L.A. Halbert *Urban Society* (New York: Thomas Y. Crowell, 1948), p. 138.

20. Sidney M. Willheld, "The Concept of the Ecological Complex: A Critique," *American Journal of Economics and Sociology* 23 (July 1964): 241-248.

21. Louis Wirth, *The Ghetto* (Chicago: University of Chicago Press, 1928), p. 285.

22. Homer Hoyt, *The Structure and Growth of Residential Neighborhoods in American Cities* (New York: Ronald Press, 1939).

23. Walter Firey, *Land Use in Central Boston* (Cambridge, Mass.: Harvard University Press, 1947).

24. See, for example: Beverly Duncan, Georges Sabagh, and Maurice D. Van Arsdol, Jr., "Patterns of City Growth," *American Journal of Sociology* 67 (January 1962): 418-429.

25. Burgess, "The Growth of a City," *The City*, p. 54.

26. Frederick Engels, *The Condition of the Working Class in London in 1844*, 3rd ed. (London: Allen and Unwin, 1962), pp. 46-47.

27. See, for example: Donald R. Deskin, Jr., *Residential Mobility of Negroes in Detroit 1837-1965* Ann Arbor: University of Michigan: Department of Geography, 1972).

28. Sylvia Fava, "Ecological Patterns Reviewed" in *Urbanism in World Perspective: Selected Readings* (New York: Thomas Y. Crowell, 1968), Introduction to Part II.

29. Herbert Blumer, "Social Science and Desegregation Process," in *Racial Desegregation and Integration*, ed. Ira De A. Reid (Philadelphia: American Academy of Political and Social Science, 1956), pp. 137-143.

30. Alvin L. Schorr, "Housing the Poor," in *Urban Poverty: Its Social and Political Dimensions*, ed. W. Bloomberg, Jr. and H.J. Schmandt (Beverly Hills, Calif: Sage Publications, 1970), p. 71.

31. John Fraser Hart, "The Changing Distribution of the American Negro," in *Black America*, ed. Robert T. Ernst and Lawrence Hugg, (New York: Anchor Books, 1976), p. 49.

32. Charles Abrams, "Invasion and Counter Attacks," in *Violence in America*, ed. Thomas Rose (New York: Vintage Books, 1970), p. 182.

33. See, for example: Charles A. Benson, "A Test of Transition Theories," *The Residential Appraiser* 24 (August 1958): 8-11.

34. Robert C. Weaver, *The Negro Ghetto* (New York: Russell Press, 1948), p. 48.

35. See, for example: H.V. Savitch, "Black Cities/White Suburbs: Domestic Colonialism As an Interpretive Idea," *Annals of the American Academy of Political and Social Science* (September 1978), pp. 118-134.

36. See, for example: Charles Abrams, *Forbidden Neighbors* (New York: Harper and Row, 1955); *Report of the United States Civil Rights Commission* (Washington, D.C.: Government Printing Office, 1959).

37. John McDermott and Dennis Clark, "Helping the Panic Neighborhood," *Interracial Review* (August 1955), pp. 30-38.

38. Davis McEntire, *Residence and Race* (Berkeley, Calif.: University of California Press, 1960), p. 159.

39. Louis K. Loewenstein, *Urban Studies* (New York: Free Press, 1971), p. 106.

40. See, for example: Herbert J. Gans, *The Urban Villagers* (New York: Free Press, 1962); Louis Seig, "Concepts of Ghetto: A Geography of Minority Groups," in *Black America*, pp. 120-125.

41. *Report of the National Advisory Commission on Civil Disorders* (Washington, D.C.: Government Printing Office, 1969).

42. See, for example: Gunnar Myrdal, *An American Dilemma* (New York: Harper and Row, 1944); Nelson N. Foote, *Housing Choices and Housing Constraints* (New York: McGraw Hill, 1960).

43. Eleanor P. Wolf, "The Tipping Point in Racially Changing Neighborhoods," *Journal of the American Institute of Planners* 29 (August 1963): 217-222; "Desegregated Housing: Who Pays for the Reformer's Ideal?" *The New Republic* 12 (December 1966), editorial, p. 1.

44. Ross K. Baker, "The Ghetto Writ Large: The Future of the American City," *Social Policy* 4 (January-February 1974): 22-29.

45. Jack Rothman, "The Ghetto Makers," in *Housing Urban America*, ed. John Pynoos, Robert Schafer, and Chester W. Hartman (Chicago: Aldine Publishing, 1973), p. 274.

46. Rose Helper, *Racial Policies and Practices of Real Estate Brokers* (Minneapolis: University of Minnesota Press, 1969).

47. See, for example: District of Columbia, *Alley Dwelling Authority*, Report of the Alley Dwelling Authority, Fiscal Years 1935-1939 (Washington, D.C.: Government Printing Office, 1936-1940); Charles Frederick Weller, *Neglected Neighbors: Stories of Life in the Alleys, Tenements and Shanties of the National Capitol* (Philadelphia: John C. Winston, 1909).

48. Constance McLaughlin Green, *The Secret City* (Princeton, N.J.: Princeton University Press, 1967), pp. 67-70.

49. Florette Henri, *Black Migration* (New York: Anchor Doubleday, 1975), p. 103.

50. Constance McLaughlin Green, *Secret City*, p. 322.

51. Anthony Downs, *Urban Problems and Prospects* (Chicago: Markham Publishing, 1971), p. 29.

52. *Displacement: City Neighborhoods in Transition* (Washington, D.C.: National Urban Coalition), introduction.

53. Interview with Virginia realtor later substantiated by articles in

Washington Post, 7 February 1978; *New York Times*, 28 June 1976; *Washington Post*, 12 July 1976.

54. Interview with Urban Institute Staff, July 1976.

55. See "Letters on Urban Revival," *New York Times* 13 July 1977.

56. Alexander Garvin, Deputy Administrator, New York City Housing and Development Administration. Speech at "Back to the City Conference" September 13, 1974.

57. *Portfolio*, a quarterly newsletter published by Walker and Dunlop, Washington, D.C. (Winter 1978), p. 1.

58. William K. Tabb and Larry Sawers, *Marxism and the Metropolis* (New York: Oxford Press, 1978).

59. David M. Gorton, *Problems in Political Economy: An Urban Perspective* (Lexington, Mass.: D.C. Heath and Company, 1971); Harvey Molotch, "The City As a Growth Machine: Toward a Political Economy of Place," *American Journal of Sociology*, 82 (September 1976): 309-332.

60. Joel Kotkin and Katherine Macdonald, "Special to the *Washington Post*," *Washington Post*, 24 July 1978.

3

Historical Development of the District of Columbia

As stated the general population trend in U.S. cities is one wherein inner cities have been gaining black population while simultaneously losing white population. The history of the District of Columbia, up to the time when private urban renewal began to make an impact, has followed this nationwide trend. The District was the first U.S. city to house a black majority population. A discussion of population composition over time shows how the city came to have such a large black population. Additionally, description of the particular areas under investigation indicates that the areas of the city that are experiencing private urban renewal are those that are or have been inhabited primarily by blacks.

Washington, or the District of Columbia, hereafter referred to as the District, is described developmentally in terms of both physical and social characteristics of the population, because the citywide attributes of the population have been used as a basis of comparison with the areas undergoing private urban renewal. Because this book is concerned with the description and explanation of a process, the historical development of the city is included in order to provide a general perspective. (See appendixes A and B for physical description).

The District is one of the national capitol cities of the world that was founded by design.[1] The idea for the designation of a site for a national capitol was put forth in 1783, when Congress was in session in Philadelphia. The location for the city was selected as a result of a compromise between the states of Virginia and Maryland. The act establishing the right to found the city was passed by Congress on July 10, 1790. The boundaries of the Federal Territory were established in 1791, and the District was designed to be ten miles square.

Division of the city into four sections—Northeast, Northwest, Southeast and Southwest—came about as a result of conscious planning wherein the two great focal points were intended to be the Capitol building and the White House. Building was intended to follow certain specified patterns; the original planning seems to have been intended to accommodate officials, foreign personnel, and other transient types associated in some manner with the federal government. The District is unique among American cities, until recently having what could be described as colonial status. As described by Ben Bagdikian:

It is a city of paradoxes. It is the least industrialized metropolis in the world, yet it often rates a "dangerous" on the scale of air pollution from motor vehicles. It is headquarters for the greatest democracy on earth, but it is denied self-government. Its most famous residents pride themselves on their benevolent leadership but Washington is the only city in modern times that has been ruled by men seemingly dedicated to the city's destruction . . .[2]

In fact, the District did have self-government for some years after its founding. In 1874 the District was politically disenfranchised. Most historians agree that the decision to disenfranchise was based on the fear that the large Negro population in the District might actually vote.[3]

Until recently the District has been presided over by four separate Congressional committees. In 1964 the passage of the Twenty-Third Amendment to the Constitution allowed District residents to vote for president and vice-president. The District can now elect nonvoting members to Congress; it has attained a modified form of Home Rule Charter, and residents can vote for mayor and City Council members. Major legislation can still be vetoed by the District Congressional Committee despite the wishes of the City Council members. The District is now awaiting ratification by the states to allow another Constitutional Amendment that would permit the sending of elected representatives to Congress.

In 1800 the District became the official seat of government, housing at that time a total population of approximately 3,000 people. On August 24, 1814 the British arrived in Washington, and the Capitol was burned. The destruction was symbolically distressing, but real property losses were few. The District, when it was burned, was comprised primarily of half-constructed buildings and unpaved streets. Between 1817 and 1825 the city was gradually rebuilt. By 1820 the total population had risen to 13,247 people. In 1835 the first railway to reach the District was completed. This provided easier access to other cities and a daily link to Baltimore.

In 1840 the resident population of the District had grown to 23,364, but the city itself was relatively undeveloped. For example, the only street lights were on Pennsylvania Avenue. It is reported that pigs wandered freely through the principal thoroughfare. It seems the situation was so distressing that there was an immediate bill introduced in Congress in the hope of moving the Capitol elsewhere, primarily because it was such a miserable backwater. However, the bill was defeated by a margin of two votes.[4]

In 1870 there was another serious proposal to move the Capitol to St. Louis, partially because the streets still had not been paved. The District was facing other difficulties by this time. It was beginning to experience an influx of approximately six thousand European immigrants; inmigration of large numbers of blacks; and a temporary "emergency" population of volunteers for the war effort who had not returned home. Public works, street paving, the laying of sidewalks, and the erecting of housing began in 1870 with seriousness of purpose. This began the era of physical building in the District, and it put the city in debt for approximately twenty million dollars.

General Population Trends

In 1800 when the District officially became the seat of government, the total population of the city was 3,210. Of this population, 1,335 were white males, 1,129 were white females, there were 623 slaves and 123 other freedmen who were black. By 1820 the population had increased to 13,247; 75 percent was white and the remainder was divided between slaves and freedmen, who were black. By 1850 the population had grown slowly. Up to this time the District had been an area of inmigration for the freedmen of Maryland and Virginia (see Appendix C).

Between 1850 and 1860 there was a sharp decline in the black population of the District. At this point the District had become an undesirable place for runaway slaves, or even freedmen, because two of its ports had numerous vessels engaged in the slave trade. The Anti-Fugitive Slave Law of 1850 was taken seriously in the District. As shown by Larry Gara, the original slave code in the District specified:

> Any free colored person coming there to reside should given the mayor satisfactory evidence of his freedom, and enter bond with two freehold sureties, in the sum of five hundred dollars for his good conduct, to be renewed each year for three years; or failing to do so, must leave the city, or be committed to the workhouse, for not more than one year, and if he still refuses to go, may be again committed for the same period, and so on.[5]

Even being able to demonstrate one's right to freedom could not prevent one from being "accidentally" apprehended. The District is in close proximity to the former major slave state of Virginia. As a result, it became an uncomfortable and sometimes dangerous place for blacks prior to the Civil War.

The black population of the District was relatively static from 1800 to 1850. Between 1850 and 1860 there was a major decline in black population. Since the end of the Civil War, the largest black migrations have taken place during periods of acute economic crises; toward the close of the depression of the 1870s; at the height of the Populist agrarian agitation around 1890; and again during the depression prior to World War I.[6] This trend is reflected in the population change in the District in the decade following the Civil War. This decade, which includes the Civil War, was one of considerable population growth in the District. Total population increased by 56 percent. During this same period the black population increased by 14 percent and the white population declined, establishing a population pattern that was to continue very gradually up to the turn of the century.

The sharp increase in black population during the decade 1860 to 1870 can be accounted for in part by the passage of the Emancipation Proclamation on September 22, 1862, effective January 1, 1863. The Proclamation accounts for increased black population in the District, because this city was one of the few wherein it could be implemented. It could not be enforced in Southern slave-holding states until the end of the Civil War and then with some difficulty. Because of the District's proximity to Southern states, it became a logical choice for migrating black populations leaving the South. Much of the black incoming population was poor, and its arrival created a serious housing shortage in the District. To solve the housing problem lots were divided, and rear portions were sold separately. In 1897 the alleys of Washington were laid out and became dwelling places for approximately 19,000 people, more than 75 percent of them Negro.[7] These alleys, much later, became the center of a series of controversial newspaper articles deploring the state of housing in the District.

Another major wave of black population migration began in the second decade of the twentieth century with peaks around World War I and World War II in 1945.[8] It is difficult to pinpoint exactly the periods of migration, because census data are collected at ten-year intervals. The migration wave after World War I did not seriously affect the population composition of the District, but the wave after World War II increased the black population by 7 percent between 1940 and 1950.

Between 1950 and 1960 a full-scale shift in population took place. Between 1900 and 1940 almost three out of four residents in the area resided in the city (72 percent). Between 1950 and 1960 only 38 percent of the total population of the metropolitan area remained in the city. Many parts of the District lost population; the areas where population increased are the outlying areas of the city. In 1960 almost 85 percent of the Negroes in the metropolitan area lived in the District. The remaining Negroes in the metropolitan area comprised only 6 percent of the total suburban population. Between 1960 and 1970 the black population of the District continued to increase, and the white population continued to decline. Although the black population of the District per se has grown rapidly over the past two decades, the proportion of blacks in the population of the entire metropolitan area had not varied—until recently—by as much as two percentage points in fifty years. The 1970 Census indicated that blacks comprise 24.6 percent of the population of the metropolitan area; 0.1 percent lower than in 1920. From 1970 to 1974 the first sign of change is recorded. During that period all the Washington metropolitan area's increase in black population went to the suburbs.[9]

In 1960 and 1970 about half of all nonwhite residents lived in census tracts, where the population was 90 percent or more nonwhite. There are also sizeable sections of the District where the population is almost entirely white. Almost all these latter tracts are located in the Northwest section of the city, which houses Georgetown, although in some respects Georgetown maintains a unique place in the city. Presently it is the primarily black census tract areas of the city that are experiencing the process of private urban renewal.

Because actual physical description is not enough to conjure up a vision of population composition, all areas of the city that are examined for the purposes of this study are described in detail. Appendix B offers a map of the physical layout of the District with the sections of the city under examination identified. These sections have been divided into restoration tracts and transition tracts where appropriate.

Cases Selected

Three separate case studies were examined for comparative purposes. The selection of this city and the particular areas within it was based on information available from popular media sources regarding private urban renewal in these locales. This is frequently the basis for selection of subareas in the study of urban sociology. For example, in his study of anomie as it exists within ghetto population, Robert Wilson studied areas undergoing racial transition. He selected the areas on a judgmental basis, because of his previous knowledge of their transitional condition.[10] This is true as well of Bonnie Bullough's study of alienation. She compares two different areas of Los Angeles, selecting the areas on the basis of her previous knowledge of residential patterns.[11] Avery Guest and James Zuiches, studying black invasion in Cleveland, utilized census boundaries for their investigation. One central question that they raise in regard to previous studies of the same phenomenon is the issue of defining appropriate geographical boundaries for study of urban areas.[12] For example, even if we accept the census tract as being the best available urban unit, how do we decide which tracts to select? The answer, according to Harvey Molotch, is that it is necessary to observe the community and to examine historical sources of data regarding the areas under examination.[13] This is the basis on which the areas of focus for this book were selected.

Information concerning the three selected locations was gathered from published historical accounts, available newspaper archives, and District government records. Other sources of available data are publications released in the particular areas. These include the Adams-Morgan Association *Newsletter*; the *In Towner*, which is a community publication; the Capitol Hill Restoration Society *Newsletter* and *Prospectus*; and historical copies of the Georgetown Citizens' Association *Newsletters*. There is a good deal of information available from newspapers, magazines, and real estate trade papers. Information concerning the private urban renewal process was also obtained through the National Society for Historical Preservation.

The three areas were selected to represent three distinct phases of the process of private urban renewal. Georgetown is the first such section of the District. It represents the most complete phase of the process. Capitol Hill was selected to represent an area in seemingly rapid transition. Adams-Morgan is a section of the District that is experiencing the beginning stages of private urban renewal. It was selected as representing the initial phase of the process. For a detailed description of the census tracts involved see appendix B.

Georgetown

The history of Georgetown[14] is not the same as the history of the District, because Georgetown has not always been a part of the city. Georgetown's history began with the development of the port of Georgetown. Here tobacco was loaded to be sent back to England. The harbor was deep enough to accommodate the early ships of that era. As a result, much trade from Europe and the West Indies was conducted from this port. Many of the original residents were Scottish businessmen, who had come to the New World for the purpose of establishing new export trade markets. They tended to be an economically affluent group whose fortunes were made before they arrived in the New World. In addition, as a thriving port city Georgetown came to accommodate many of the officials of the U.S. government as well as foreign dignitaries.

Settlement of Georgetown began in the early eighteenth century. During the early years of the Republic it was believed that it might develop to a point where it would compete with New York and Philadelphia for preeminence along the Eastern seaboard. In its early days it had gun factories and important docks along with other industries. Its original housing was built by wealthy planters and merchants, whose businesses required that they utilize the port. At the same time, these people were building barns for tobacco storage and rear location slave quarters. Between 1785 and 1825 Georgetown grew rapidly; its tobacco inspection stop and its port were considered the best in Maryland, if not the entire United States. During this period Georgetown was at the pinnacle of its development. But it began to experience difficulty and rivalry with other ports because of the building of large ships that could not be accommodated in the harbor. In 1871 the Charter of the City of Georgetown was revoked and it became officially part of the District of Columbia. The decree by Congress came in 1895. In this year the final steps were taken to integrate it with the rest of the city.

By the time Georgetown was made an integral part of the District its decline was already underway. With the advent of the railroad and the need for a deeper harbor it lost importance as a commercial port. The waterfront had fallen into disuse. At the time of annexation Georgetown had deteriorated into a shabby neighborhood dotted with large mansions. By 1900 many of the smaller old houses in the area, including the barns and former slave quarters, were rented to black families who made up approximately 4,000 of its 15,000 residents. In 1930 more than 40 percent of the residents of Georgetown were black, poor, and living in substandard housing without benefit of water and/or electricity. In the late 1930s the District experienced a severe housing shortage.

It was sometime during this period that the process of private urban renewal began.

Capitol Hill

Capitol Hill[15] is the residential area which lies in front of the Capitol building. Actually, the Capitol faces East, and not toward the Mall, which is the common supposition. Defining the boundaries of this area is not as clear-cut a task as is the case of Georgetown. For example, the Capitol Hill Restoration Society, whose partial purpose is to obtain historical preservation status for the area, has changed its boundaries several times. The government of the District had once included it in a much larger total Service Area. Service Areas were then changed to coincide with the city's eight election wards. Realtors appear to define the area in terms of the private urban renewal process. That is, as the process spreads, so do the areas designated Capitol Hill.

Capitol Hill is, under any circumstances, one of the largest residential areas in the District. The history of development of this area parallels, to a large extent, the development of the city in general. The majority of the housing in the area and the most extensive growth of population came about during and immediately after the Civil War. The majority of the housing in the area was built for middle-class families. In the original plan for the city, l'Enfant projected a view of the area around the Capitol as a fashionable residential area and one that would provide convenient housing for those who worked for the federal government.

In approximately 1800 some fashionable houses were built in the area. However, the District grew to the North and West and not to the East of the Capitol, as had been foreseen. The end result is that most of the houses built in the area were for the middle class rather than the very rich. The area does have a number of mansions scattered throughout, but these are the exception rather than the rule.

Capitol Hill is an area of the city that came to house several ethnic communities by 1900. The original ethnic composition of the area was primarily Italian, German, and Irish. There are still some families of ethnic stock who have remained in the area despite other population changes.

The original black population of this area was small and consisted of a group of freedmen. This population remained in the area and continued to be a small proportion of the population up until the 1930s, when the black rural population began to migrate to the cities. The first major population change affecting the area occurred in approximately 1920 with the advent of the automobile. With this development the more affluent moved to the periphery of the city and into the suburbs.

During the course of the Depression the federal government purchased

some houses Northeast of the Capitol and rented them to poor families. This
increased the wave of outmigration of the more affluent. In 1948 a series of
articles appeared in various magazines depicting the squalor and deterioration
of the area surrounding the front of the Capitol. One of the more notorious
of these essays is written about Schott's Alley. This alley was apparently of
particularly poor quality, since the various residences along it lacked even the
minimum city requirement of indoor plumbing.

In 1948 the population of the Capitol Hill area consisted primarily of low-
income blacks. What had its beginning as a white, middle-class area with some
ethnic pockets dispersed within it, had, by 1948, deteriorated to the point
wherein the area was being nationally declared a slum in the backyard of the
Capitol. Actually this is incorrect, it is the frontyard.

Adams-Morgan

The area comprising the Adams-Morgan[16] community has been know as such,
with minor boundary changes, since the nineteenth century. It is located in
Northwest Washington, between Sixteenth Street on the East and Connecticut
Avenue on the West. Harvard Street is the northern boundary, and Florida
Avenue and R Streets enclose the southern end.

In 1750, fifty years before the District became the nation's Capitol, the
first manor estate was built by the nephew of George Washington and was
called "Kalorama." This estate was built about three-quarters of a mile from the
heart of downtown Washington and was the center of the area that came to be
known as Adams-Morgan. Later many more of Washington's statesmen and
diplomats built large brick houses in this area. For example, six Presidents of
the United States lived in Adams-Morgan either before or after their terms of
office. Up until 1930 this area of the city remained a fashionable and expensive
section of the District.

The major changes in Adams-Morgan began during and immediately following World War II. As previously mentioned, during this period there was a
general housing shortage in the District and a large increase in population. Many
of the larger houses in the Adams-Morgan area were subdivided into rooming
houses. This section of the city has a large number of apartment buildings,
which were also subdivided to accommodate the large incoming population.
The availability of apartment houses has made this section of the city one where
large numbers of immigrant groups have settled. For example, Adams-Morgan
currently houses the largest Spanish-speaking community in the District.

As of 1960 approximately 20 percent of all the households in the area
were at or below the poverty level. According to District standards there is
approximately 10 percent overcrowding in housing. At present it appears that
the area is undergoing a process of deterioration—if analysis is based exclusively

on available census statistics. If the three areas, Georgetown, Capitol Hill, and Adams-Morgan are compared mechanically, there are insufficient data to indicate changes in Adams-Morgan. However, there is evidence that private urban renewal is beginning in this area as well. This will be discussed at length in the following chapters.

Notes

1. Unless otherwise indicated the material describing the general historical development of the District of Columbia is derived from the following sources: Charles Moore, *Washington Past and Present* (New York: Century Company, 1929); Wilhelmust Bogart Bryan, comp., *Bibliography of the District of Columbia: Being a List of Maps, and Newspapers, Including Articles in Other Publications to 1898* (Washington, D.C.: Government Printing Office, 1900); *Records of the Columbia Historical Society* (Washington, D.C.: Columbia Historical Society, 1895-1973); Constance McLaughlin Green, *Washington: Village and Capital, 1800-1878* (Princeton, N.J.: Princeton University Press, 1962).

2. Ben Bagdikian, "The Five Different Washingtons," in *Washington: A Reader* ed. Bill Adler (New York. Meredith Press, 1967), p. 260.

3. See, for example: George Edmund Haynes, *The American Negro* (New York: Arno Press and the New York Times, 1969).

4. Adler, *Washington: A Reader* p. 261.

5. Larry Gara, *The Library Line* (Lexington, Ky.: University of Kentucky Press, 1969), p. 81.

6. George A. Davis and O. Fred Donaldson, *Blacks in the United States: A Geographic Perspective* (Boston: Houghton Mifflin, 1975), p. 6.

7. Letitia Woods Brown, *Free Negroes in the District of Columbia 1790-1846* (New York: Oxford University Press, 1972), p. 220.

8. Davis and Donaldson, *Blacks in the United States*, p. 38.

9. Statistics for the periods 1950 to 1960 and 1960 to 1970 have been compiled from: Eunice S. Grier, *Understanding Washington's Changing Population* (Washington, D.C.: Washington Center Metropolitan Studies, 1961); 1970 Census of Population, *General Population Characteristics* (Washington, D.C.: Government Printing Office); Eunice and George Grier, "Black Suburbanization at the Mid-1970's," Washington Center for Metropolitan Studies (April 1978) p. 6.

10. Robert A. Wilson, "Anomie in the Ghetto: A Study of Neighborhood Type, Race and Anomie," *American Journal of Sociology* 77 (November 1971): 66-87.

11. Bonnie Bullough, "Alienation in the Ghetto," *American Journal of Sociology* 72 (March 1967): 469-478.

12. Avery M. Guest and James J. Zuiches, "Another Look at Residential Turnover in Urban Neighborhoods: A Note on 'Racial Change in a Stable Community by Harvey Molotch,'" *American Journal of Sociology* 77 (November 1971): 458.

13. Harvey Molotch, "Reply to Guest and Zuiches: Another Look at Residential Turnover in Urban Neighborhoods," *American Journal of Sociology* 77 (November 1971): 468.

14. Unless otherwise indicated, the material on Georgetown was derived from the following sources: Grace Dunlop Ecker, *A Portrait of Old Georgetown* (Richmond: Garrett and Massie, 1933); S. Somervell Mackall, *Early Days of Washington* (Washington, D.C.: Peabody Collection, 1899); portfolios of Washington Neighborhoods, Martin Luther King Library, Washingtonian Room, Washington, D.C.

15. Unless otherwise indicated, the material on Capitol Hill has been derived from the following sources: Records of the Capitol Hill Restoration Society; Paul Herron, *The Story of Capitol Hill* (New York: Coward McCann, 1963); Lewis Mumford, *The City in History: Its Origins, Its Transformations, and Its Prospects* (New York: Harcourt, Brace and World, 1961).

16. Unless otherwise indicated, the material on Adams-Morgan has been derived from the following sources: District of Columbia Public Library System, Peabody Room; *Preliminary Demographic Profile II,* Urban Studies Program, Howard University, 1970; past records of the *In Towner.*

4

Dynamics of Private Urban Renewal

Measuring Change in Population

The first question to be considered is to what extent private urban renewal involves a change in the population composition of the areas under examination. To answer this question a number of social attributes of the population were examined. This was undertaken in an effort to determine (1) whether the characteristics of the population in private urban renewal areas change in a similar manner, and (2) whether or not there are patterns of change at similar time intervals.

The steps that were accomplished in analyzing residential population change are as follows:

1. The exact number of census tracts involved in the three areas was established (see Appendix B). This was based on city government demarkation guidelines.

2. A census of population and housing was collected as part of the decennial censuses of 1940, 1950, 1960, and 1970. Because these censuses have comparable categories they were utilized to describe population at the time intervals specified. In addition to national census data, where more current data are available the information has been updated.

3. In some of the categories the numbers were converted to percentages.

4. The current population of the three areas is described from data obtained from interviews with key personnel in local organizations, interviews with realtors, popular media sources, and property value information. This material does not describe population changes with the same precision as do census data. However, it does indicate a continuing trend in the areas under examination.

General Population Trends

An analysis of the general population trends in Georgetown, Capitol Hill, and Adams-Morgan was undertaken at ten-year intervals between 1940 and 1970 and for the years between 1970 and 1975. As indicated in table 4-1, it can be shown that as the process of private urban renewal takes place, population within the affected areas declines. For example, in 1940 the total population of Georgetown was 8,278 and 6,680 in census tracts one and two respectively. Between 1940 and 1950, the total population of the District increased by 139,087 or

Table 4-1
Population Trends in Private Urban Renewal Areas and Citywide, 1940-1975

	Population				
	1940	1950	1960	1970	1975
Citywide	663,091	802,178	763,956	756,510	721,800
Location and tract numbers					
Georgetown					
1	8,278	7,658	5,963	5,480	5,200
2	6,680	6,071	5,723	5,974	5,200
Adams-Morgan					
38	5,714	6,220	5,173	5,200	4,200
39	5,099	5,643	5,325	6,100	4,900
40	8,528	9,137	7,599	7,289	6,400
Capitol Hill					
65	7,057	6,806	4,730	3,700	2,900
66	4,311	4,057	3,004	2,268	1,600
67	7,028	6,938	6,850	5,733	5,200
70	6,779	6,970	5,973	3,133	2,600
81	5,021	5,280	5,599	4,711	4,400
82	6,903	6,473	4,217	2,996	2,200

Source: Statistics were collected from the following sources: *Population and Housing Statistics for Census Tracts* (Washington, D.C.: U.S. Bureau of Commerce, 1942), table 1, p. 4.; *Census Tract Statistics, Washington and Adjacent Areas* (Washington, D.C.: U.S. Bureau of Commerce, 1952), table 1, p. 7; *United States Census of Population and Housing* (Washington, D.C.: U.S. Bureau of Commerce, 1961), p. 16; *United States Census of Population and Housing, General Characteristics of the Population* (Washington, D.C.: U.S. Bureau of Commerce, 1972), p. 8.; Government of the District of Columbia, Municipal Planning Office, *Population Estimates, 1975*, May 1977.

21 percent. During this same time interval, Georgetown, which was in the beginning stage of the private urban renewal process, experienced a decline in total population of 1,229 or 8 percent. While the entire city was undergoing a major increase in population, Georgetown was in the process of population decline.

Between 1950 and 1960 the total population of the District experienced a decline from 802,178 to 763,956. The population of Georgetown declined again in total population, this time by 14 percent. This is contrasted to a citywide decline of 5 percent for the same time interval. This is a substantial decline, considering that Georgetown is comprised of two relatively small census tracts.

Between 1960 and 1970 the city again experienced a population decrease from 763,956 to 756,510 or a 1 percent loss. The total population of Georgetown decreased by 4 percent during this time. As a general population trend, the private urban renewal area of Georgetown steadily has lost population over time. The most dramatic losses are in the earlier period, when the process of private urban renewal was in its beginning stages, but the pattern of decrease in population was maintained over the time periods under examination, and the decreases remain steadily larger than that of the citywide population decreases for the same time intervals.

The Capitol Hill area is not geographically as neat as Georgetown. Moreover, all the census tracts are not equally affected by the private urban renewal process. Six census tracts have been included in this analysis. It is difficult to describe with complete accuracy the population changes in this area between 1940 and 1950, because there was some shifting of census boundaries during that period. In general, there was a slight loss of population in nearly every tract during this period, but these losses may be a result of boundary shifts. As previously mentioned, between 1950 and 1960 the total population of the District declined by 5 percent. This trend is reflected in every census tract but one on Capitol Hill. It is likely that this population decline can be accounted for by the general loss of citywide population during this period. The area began to manifest differences from the citywide trend between 1960 and 1970. During this decade the District population declined by 1 percent of total population. It is during this period that the private urban renewal process began to gain momentum on Capitol Hill.

The entire area of Capitol Hill lost 7,832 people or 26 percent of its total population between 1960 and 1970. A tract-by-tract examination shows that population loss was as high as 36 percent in the census tracts Southeast of the Capitol; there was a range from 28 percent to 15 percent in the other tracts. This pattern is maintained through 1975 with losses ranging from 7 percent to 29 percent across tracts.

The Adams-Morgan area is at the very beginning stages of the process of private urban renewal. Up to 1970 analysis of census data leads to the conclusion that the process was not well enough underway to be strongly indicated in the general population trends. For example, the historical development of Adams-Morgan has reflected the development of the entire city. Between 1940 and 1950 it increased in population in proportion to the remainder of the city. Between 1950 and 1960 there was a loss of population in all three tracts, which is in keeping with the citywide loss. Between 1960 and 1970 there was only a 4 percent population loss in one tract in the area. The dramatic population loss began after 1970, and as of 1975 the population declined by 12 to 19 percent across tracts. This is compared to a citywide loss of 4.6 percent for the same period.

Race

As indicated in table 4-1, as the process of private urban renewal takes place, population declines in affected areas. Changes are manifested in racial

osition of the population as well (see appendixes C and D).[1] Data on race
n have been used to examine black invasion of white areas. The findings of
ese studies are fairly consistent: once an area begins to be invaded by a black
population, it ultimately becomes an extension of the ghetto.[2] It is equally
possible that when a white population invades an area it may rapidly spread and
expand throughout the area. The category of race was examined over the time
periods previously specified in order to determine whether or not this reverse
pattern operates.

In 1940 the total population of the District was 663,091; 72 percent white
and 28 percent black. The black population in Georgetown's census tracts
ranged from 14 percent to 28 percent. Between 1940 and 1950 the total population of the District increased by 139,087. This represents an increase in black
population of 93,537 or 7 percent citywide. At this time the black population
in Georgetown was on the decline, with census tracts in 1950 indicating the
black population at 8 percent and 17 percent. While the entire city was undergoing an increase in total population and an increase in percentage of black
population, Georgetown was declining in total population; simultaneously there
was a sharp decrease of its black population as well.

Between 1950 and 1960 the black percentage of the population in the
District increased from 35 percent to 55 percent; an overall increase wherein
blacks became a majority of the citywide population. Again, the black population of the District was rising, while Georgetown experienced a further decrease
in black population. This reduced the black population of Georgetown to the
1 percent to 5 percent range. By 1970 the population of Georgetown had
steadily decreased and had, as of 1970, a total black population of approximately 2 percent.

In Capitol Hill the population trend in regard to racial composition over
time has followed the citywide trend. As the racial composition of the city
has changed and the black population has increased, Capitol Hill has reflected
this type of change up to 1960. Between 1950 and 1960 the District experienced a dramatic population change. First, the total population declined by
38,222 or 5 percent. At the same time 172,602 white population members left
the District while 134,380 blacks entered. It was during this period that the
share of the black population of the District increased by 50 percent in a ten-
year interval. Most of the census tracts on Capitol Hill reflect the citywide
change ranging from a 20 percent to 100 percent increase in black population
across tracts.

Between 1960 and 1970 the black population of the District continued
to increase, and the white population continued to decrease. As of the 1970
census, the racial composition of the District was 72 percent black and 28 percent white; a total reversal in racial composition since 1940. Between 1960 and
1970 the black population in the Capitol Hill census tracts in the Southeast and
close to the U.S. Capitol declined significantly, whereas the further out tracts

and the tracts located in the Northeast indicated less significant decreases in this population. The process of private urban renewal had its beginning in Capitol Hill at a later time than in Georgetown, but the patterns of population change are similar. These similarities are manifested in both total population and racial composition of the area. In every census tract on Capitol Hill there has been some decline in total population, but as the total citywide population became increasingly black, the areas in the Southeast and close to the Capitol building lost a substantial proportion of black population.

In Adams-Morgan the census data to 1970 appear to predate the private urban renewal phenomenon in all but one census tract, wherein there is a substantial loss of black population. However, the total population of the area has declined four times faster than the citywide decline for the same period, 1970 to 1975.

There are no reliable statistics concerning race by census tract after 1970. At least there are no data available that are comparable in accuracy to the U.S. census material. However, it is possible to conclude that there is racial change in private urban renewal areas by extrapolating from other available information. For example, in 1977 a survey of recent homebuyers was conducted in two census tracts of Capitol Hill. The households in the study area were overwhelmingly composed of whites (94 percent).[3] The percentage of blacks in the District has been declining over the past four years. Since 1970 more than 27,000 blacks left the city for an average annual decline more than double that of whites. It is presumed by most analysts that these figures reflect the changes in the private urban renewal areas of the District.[4]

Income

Census tract data are limited because of the inability to crosstabulate variables. Because of this limitation, some social attributes have been examined independently. Median income of families was examined for the periods when these data are available. Appendix E indicates the median income of families in the census tracts examined, as well as the citywide median income of families for the same periods.[5] This information was not collected in the 1940 census. Numbers were rounded to the nearest hundred dollars. They have not been adjusted for inflation on the assumption that inflation affects all tracts equally and is reflected in the citywide figures. Despite the fact that there has been inflation over time, the information has internal consistency.

Over time populations in most private urban renewal tracts have become disproportionately affluent. For example, in 1950 the median family income in Georgetown was lower than the citywide median for the same period. By 1960 the median family income of Georgetown was $4600 above the citywide median; by 1970 it was more than double that of the median family income for the city as a whole.

In 1950 the median family income on Capitol Hill was lower than the city-wide median for the same period. A similar pattern is indicated in the 1960 census data; the median family income was lower than the citywide median. By 1970 the changes in Capitol Hill were beginning to emerge. In two of the census tracts of Capitol Hill the median family income increased by $3400 above the citywide median; in a third tract the increase was $4600 above the citywide figure.

In Adams-Morgan in 1950 all tracts were below the citywide median income. In 1960 two were equal to the citywide figure, and by 1970 only one tract was on a level with the citywide median income level.

Between 1970 and 1975, 41,200 people moved into the District. Whites strongly predominate this population. Sixteen percent of this new population has moved into the area of the city that contains Adams-Morgan; nine percent of this population has moved into the Capitol Hill area. Twenty-eight percent of this population indicates incomes between $15,000 and $24,999. Eleven per-cent of this new white population has an income of $25,000 or more.[6]

Education

The category of median years of school completed for persons twenty-five years old and over was examined primarily to add a dimension to the description of the population in private urban renewal areas (see appendix F).[7] In 1940 in Georgetown, median years of school completed was below the city-wide median for the same period. By 1950 it had risen to where it was slightly above the citywide median. Between 1950 and 1960 the citywide median educational level dropped, probably because of the loss of white population during this period. At this point Georgetown was three to four years above the citywide median in both census tracts.

The trend in median educational level in Capitol Hill was equal to or below the citywide median in every tract in 1940. By 1950 all the census tracts of Capitol Hill were below the citywide median. In 1960 two census tracts on Capitol Hill were slightly above the citywide median, the higher of the two being the census tract most closely located to the Capitol building. The remainder of the tracts were equal to or below the citywide median. Between 1960 and 1970 three census tracts had gained in median educational level by 1.5 to 2 years. The tracts on Capitol Hill that have increased to the point where they are above the citywide median are the same tracts where income has risen considerably above the citywide median and the population has changed from black to white.

In 1940 the Adams-Morgan census tracts were above the citywide median educational level. This pattern was maintained through 1950 and 1960, although the median educational level in the area declined between 1950 and 1960 within tracts. In 1970 one census tract in Adams-Morgan had fallen below the citywide median, although it had risen from its median in 1960. The other two tracts were slightly above the citywide median by 1970.

As previously stated, a substantial number of white people moved into Capitol Hill and Adams-Morgan between 1970 and 1975. Data available to 1974 indicate that 72 percent of the white population new to the District has attained at least a college level of education. In addition, 55 percent of this white population is employed in professional/technical and/or managerial/administrative work.[8]

Changes in Residential Use

Examining population changes in terms of social attributes in the private urban renewal areas of the District demonstrates that certain changes are taking place. The second question is: To what extent does the process of private urban renewal involve changes in residential use, housing conditions, and property values? Owner and renter occupancy has been examined to determine whether areas experiencing this process are characterized by an increase in "owner occupancy."[9] Further, owner occupancy has been examined in regard to the attribute "race."[10] This latter category is included because the general population trend indicates that as an area begins and proceeds to undergo private urban renewal, the racial composition of the affected area becomes increasingly white. Renter occupancy has been examined as well in order to add another dimension to the analysis.

Owner Occupancy in Private Urban Renewal Areas

Between 1940 and 1950, home ownership in the District increased citywide as well as in the areas under investigation. This increase refers to the category of owner-occupied dwellings and not to ownership in general (see appendixes G and H). During this period the citywide owner occupied rate increased by approximately 39 percent. Georgetown, in the process of private urban renewal, increased in owner occupied units by almost 50 percent. In fact, owner occupancy increased in every census tract included in this investigation over the same period, which is in keeping with the citywide trend.

Between 1950 and 1960 owner occupancy in the District continued to grow, but at a less rapid pace than during the preceding decade. For example, between 1940 and 1950, the owner-occupied population increased by 39 percent; between 1950 and 1960 it increased by only 4 percent. Georgetown during the latter period increased its owner-occupied population by 20 percent and 7 percent respectively in the first and second tracts. At this time the owner-occupied population of Georgetown increased at a rate considerably higher than the citywide rate for the same period. Between 1960 and 1970 home ownership in Georgetown stabilized, while citywide it decreased by approximately 2,000 units.

Capitol Hill experienced a decline in total owner-occupied population during the period 1950-1960. Historical records of the Restoration Society indicate that the population loss during this period was as a result of the 1954 School Desegregation decision.[11] Between 1960 and 1970 the census tracts close to the Capitol gained homeowners, while the further out tracts decreased along with the rest of the city. In the Adams-Morgan section the owner-occupied population increased in all census tracts through 1960 and dropped in 1970.

The breakdown in black and white owner occupancy patterns renders better information regarding the process of private urban renewal. For example, in Georgetown over the time periods indicated (1940-1970), there is an enormous turnover in black/white owner occupancy patterns. In both census tracts of Georgetown the black owner-occupied population steadily declined between 1940 and 1970 while the white homeowning population steadily increased, almost doubling during the thirty-year period. Even in 1970, when there is a slight loss in owner occupancy in one census tract, the white owner-occupied population amounts to 97 percent of the total population of the area.

In the restoration and transition tracts of Capitol Hill between 1940 and 1960 the white owner-occupied population declined in all but one census tract. Between 1960 and 1970 when the process of private urban renewal was underway, the black owner-occupied population declined in every tract; the black owner-occupied population decline began between 1950 and 1960 in the tracts closest to the Capitol. Between 1960 and 1970 this pattern spread to other tracts.

The owner-occupied population of Adams-Morgan had steadily increased up to 1960. Between 1960 and 1970 black owner occupancy had decreased by more than one-third in two census tracts. White owner occupancy was still decreasing through 1970 yet at a much slower pace than the citywide figures.

Between 1970 and 1974 whites strongly predominated among the newcomers to the District (63 percent). Most of this population located in areas undergoing private urban renewal or in the section of the city West of the Park. Moreover, virtually all recent homebuyers who were newcomers to the District were white, and most of this population purchased houses valued considerably above the citywide median price at this time.[12] A 1977 survey of homebuyers on Capitol Hill indicates that households were overwhelmingly composed of whites.[13] Analysis of home ownership patterns in private urban renewal areas leads to the conclusion that as the process proceeds there is a general increase in the owner-occupied population, a decrease in the black owner-occupied population, and a simultaneous increase in the white owner-occupied group.

Renter Occupancy

Another indicator selected to provide a trend analysis of change in residential use is the category of renter population. All occupied units that are not classified as owner occupied are counted as renter occupied. The citywide pattern between 1940 and 1970 indicates a fairly consistent drop in white renters and a fairly consistent pattern of increase of black renters. That is, the white renter population has decreased by 26 percent, while the black renter population has increased by 155 percent.

Population changes in Georgetown over this period (1940 to 1970) have been quite different from the rest of the city. Between 1940 and 1970, while the city was increasing in black renter population, Georgetown decreased its black renter population to the point where only 2.5 percent of the current renter population is black. The most substantial changes in the black renter population occurred between 1940 and 1950, when the area was in the initial stages of private urban renewal. During this time interval Georgetown lost 22 percent of its black renter population. This was at a time when the citywide renter population was relatively stable. During the period 1950 to 1960 the citywide figures indicate a substantial loss in white renter population, but the white renter population of Georgetown continued to increase, while there was a 13 percent loss of black renter population. As stated, this trend continued to 1970, when the renter population of Georgetown was 97 percent white (see appendix I).

There was some loss of white renter population in almost every census tract on Capitol Hill between 1940 and 1950, but the major population changes occurred between 1950 and 1960 in this area. Although losses in some of these tracts were as low as 5 percent, in the majority of the tracts on Capitol Hill the loss in white renter population was closer to 40 percent. Between 1960 and 1970 there was another population change in renter-occupied units. For example, census tract number 65 showed a loss of black renters of approximately 16 percent; this is true of census tract 70 as well. Significantly the major increase in black renters on Capitol Hill occurs in the decade between 1950 and 1960. Between 1960 and 1970 this trend has either slowed or reversed.

Between 1940 and 1970, in census tracts 38 and 39 of Adams-Morgan there was a consistent pattern of loss in white renter population. This is in keeping with the citywide trend. This is not the case in census tract forty. That tract has a loss of white renter population of 11 percent from 1940 to 1960. Between 1960 and 1970 the reduction in white renter population was only 4 percent in tract 40, whereas tracts 38 and 39 as well as citywide losses are at the 50 percent level.

In comparing these data to the ownership data, it would appear that home ownership is a lead indicator of a neighborhood in transition. A review of certain census tracts between 1960 and 1970 shows an upswing in home ownership by whites, while the renter population seems to remain stable or in some cases the white percentage of renters may even drop. This phenomenon may have a plausible explanation. One possibility is that the private urban renewal population is a home-purchasing population that buys and/or restores for personal use. The consequence of this is two-fold. First, there is no sizeable new renting population in the early stages of the process and second, one might presume that large apartment buildings tend to remain stable in their population composition and are more than likely the last structures to be restored.

Changes in Property Value

Median value by census tract was analyzed using the citywide median value as a basis for comparison. The purpose of examining these data was to investigate whether the process of private urban renewal involves changes in property values? As indicated in table 4-2, the median value of property in the District increased by 91 percent between 1940 and 1950. The period 1950 to 1960 represents a much lower rate of appreciation in median property value citywide—a drop of 6 percent. The slower appreciation growth is probably accountable to the citywide population loss during this period, particularly the decrease in white population. This was obviously a period of flux in the District as a whole, and the uncertainty of the general situation is reflected in the property values during this interval. This is in keeping with the literature concerning property values, which suggests that in times of rapid population transition, residential prices tend to drop, at least temporarily. The citywide increase in property value for the period 1950-1960 was less than $10,000. This is a particularly low figure when contrasted to the appreciation of the preceding decade wherein property value had doubled.

In Georgetown in 1940, one census tract was slightly above the citywide median. The other tract showed a median property value of $25,000 above the citywide median value. Between 1940 and 1950 the median property value of Georgetown increased in close approximation to the citywide increase—that is, 100 percent. The other tract appreciated by 63 percent during the same period.

In 1940 the median property value in every Capitol Hill census tract was below the citywide median. Between 1940 and 1950 all these census tracts doubled in median property value, in keeping with the citywide rate of appreciation. Between 1950 and 1960 these same tracts increased slightly in median

Table 4-2
Median Value by Census Tract and Citywide, Including Percentage Changes between Decades, 1940–1970[a]

Time	City	Georgetown		Capitol Hill						Adams-Morgan		
		1	2	65	66	67	70	81	82	38	39	40
1940	75	100	76	60	70	60	46	57	67	67	86	120
1950	145	200	120	130	130	120	90	120	120	–	170	190
1940-1950	91	100	63	100	85	100	96	110	90	–	97	58
1960	154	250	250	150	180	130	117	129	165	133	115	164
1950-1960	6	25	125	38	38	6	38	7	27	–	-33	-14
1970	282	500+	500+	330	360	233	302	178	330	175	235	407
1960-1970	83	100	100	120	100	79	158	38	100	31	104	148

Source: *Population and Housing Statistics for Census Tracts, Value of Owner-Occupancy Dwelling Units*, table 5 (Washington, D.C.: Government Printing Office, 1941), pp. 26-42; U.S. *Census Population*, Vol. III, Chapter 69, table 3 (Washington, D.C.: U.S. Government Printing Office, 1950); U.S. *Census of Population and Housing, Final Report*, table H-2 (Washington, D.C.: U.S. Government Printing Office, 1961), pp. 180-185; *Census of Population and Housing*, (Washington, D.C.: U.S. Government Printing Office, 1970) pp. H:1-11.

[a]Numbers are calculated in hundreds.

property value. Four of these census tracts increased by at least $20,000, compared to the citywide $10,000. In percentages, when the citywide appreciation was 6 percent for the decade, four of the Capitol Hill tracts increased by a range of 6 to 38 percent. Since these are the same tracts that later (1960-1970) show changes in social attributes of the population, it is likely that speculation in property began earlier (1950-1960) and manifested in an increase in property value before changes in population characteristics were manifested.

In 1940 the median value of property was different in every census tract of Adams-Morgan. One tract was slightly below the citywide median, one was slightly above, and one was considerably above. Between 1940 and 1950, there was an increase equal to the citywide increase in one census tract and an increase slightly lower in the other. Between 1950 and 1960 there was a considerable decrease in property value in these same two tracts—in one $39,000 less than citywide changes over the decade. This was a period wherein the total population in these tracts declined and black population increased.

Between 1960 and 1970 median value of property in the District increased sharply; the increase was $12,800 or 83 percent. The median property value of Georgetown in both tracts had increased to more than $50,000, nearly double the citywide increase. Four of the census tracts of Capitol Hill, in this period, increased in median property value by at least $2,000 and by as much as $8,000 above the citywide gain. These numbers represent an increase of 100 to 158 percent compared to a citywide increase of 83 percent over the same decade.

In Adams-Morgan, between 1960 and 1970, two tracts increased dramatically in median value. Increases are by $12,000 and $24,000 respectively, representing a percentage increase of 104 and 148 percent. This again is contrasted to the citywide appreciation of 83 percent. Thus, Adams-Morgan not only made up for the loss in median property value experienced between 1950 and 1960, it increased considerably more than citywide increase for this same time.

Sales Price and Sales Activity post-1970

It is ordinarily assumed that when a neighborhood changes the composition of the population of the area manifests the first signs of change. What is being suggested by the use of sales price and sales activity is that these variables can be utilized to indicate neighborhood change before changes in the population manifest. These data show interesting patterns emerging in private urban renewal areas.

As indicated in table 4-3, citywide data concerning median sales price of residential dwelling units show an 80 percent increase between 1971 and 1976. Interestingly enough, this is the same increase citywide for the entire decade 1960 to 1970.

Table 4-3
Median Sales Price and Sales Activity by Census Tract, post-1970

Census Tracts	1971		1976		Percentage Increase in Value
	Price	Activity	Price	Activity	
Georgetown					
1	73,000	103	145,000	63	99
2	65,000	77	133,000	81	105
Capitol Hill					
65	44,000	65	76,000	53	73
66	44,000	57	83,000	49	89
67	32,000	96	69,000	122	115
70	36,000	58	70,000	59	94
81	22,000	47	55,000	81	150
82	42,000	56	80,000	54	90
Adams-Morgan					
38	16,800	13	30,000	26	79
39	21,000	18	54,000	28	157
40	38,000	31	82,000	32	115
Citywide	29,000		52,000		80

Source: Data made available by the Municipal Planning Office of the Government of the
District of Columbia, 1977.

Within this period (1971-1976) sales prices have increased in Georgetown
between 99 percent and 105 percent. This is the same value increase in Georgetown between 1960 and 1970. Additionally, this price increase is approximately
25 percent more than the citywide figure. As to sales activity, there is a decline
in one census tract and a stable sales activity pattern in the other. From these
data it appears that Georgetown has stabilized into a neighborhood that is in
great demand.

In Capitol Hill, where 1960 to 1970 increases in median price ranged from
38 to 120 percent, the data for 1976 indicate that the rate of increase from
1971 to 1976 ranges from 73 to 150 percent. These higher increases no longer
tend to be in the tracts close to the Capitol, although those tracts represent the
highest values in the area. Sales activity in the tracts close to the Capitol repeat
a pattern found in Georgetown. That is, a stabilization or decrease in sales
activity has occurred. In the tracts that are in transition, sales activity is on the
increase, and correspondingly higher median price increases are manifested
when compared to the stable tracts.

In Adams-Morgan the 1976 increases range from 79 to 157 percent. Like
Capitol Hill, the prime tract (40) has higher sales values than the other tracts
in the area. Sales volume indicates that tract 40 has stabilized. The other two

tracts have indicated substantial increase in sales activity. However, in tract 38 the price increase was the same as the citywide increase, and tract 39 had double the citywide increase. Utilization of these two variables, sales price and sales activity, is discussed at length in the final chapter.

Realtors' Perceptions of the Private Urban Renewal Process

To confirm the data that are available from census tract reports and to update information concerning private urban renewal areas, interviews were conducted with realtors between 1975 and late 1976. This information was used to address the question of how private urban renewal is initiated and continued. Much of the information pertaining to this question can be obtained from an examination of existing records, newspaper reports, archives of local community organizations, and other popular media sources. However, it is frequently suggested in the literature that realtors are a pivotal part of neighborhood change. It is suggested additionally that their role in the process of change should be examined, although this is infrequently accomplished.[14] Because they are perceived as important participants in private urban renewal, interviews were conducted. Data obtained through interviews are discussed in this chapter as well as in the next two chapters (see appendix J for a discussion of sampling techniques and a description of the respondents).

Deirdre Stanforth and Martha Stamm, in their book, *Buying and Renovating a House in the City*, claim that "The renovation movement has given birth to a new breed of real estate brokers, who live in the community in which they sell and have a stake in its development; in many cases, these are the renovators turned brokers."[15] This appears to be the case for the realtors interviewed. Most of the respondents indicate that they live in the city; a substantial proportion live in private urban renewal areas. They further indicated that most of the staff of the various offices lives in the city. Many of the respondents indicated that the restoration business is different from what they described as "routine real estate sales jobs." The reason given for this assertion is that there is commitment to inner city renewal, and one has to be in a position to know the area well before one can attempt to promote it. All the respondents cited money as their primary reason for entering the real estate business. A substantial number of these people had already bought and/or restored and sold a house in a private urban renewal area before going to work in the business. They mentioned this experience as being a motivating factor for entering real estate sales when they did.

One of the most interesting findings as a result of these interviews is the high degree of consistency of response. This is not intended to make any claim regarding the validity of responses, since, as in all interview situations, there is some question of accuracy of perceptions on the part of the respondents.

However, there was almost total agreement in terms of stated perceptions of the respondents concerning the private urban renewal process. The interview schedule was structured and formal, and all respondents were asked exactly the same questions as well as given the same probes. Some of the topics covered in the questions were considered to be somewhat sensitive, because of the political conflicts regarding the process of private urban renewal that were taking place. These conflicts are discussed at length in chapter 6. Aware of this possible area of sensitivity, two different interviewers were used, and an attempt was made to conduct the interviews simultaneously. This was arranged in an effort to avoid allowing the respondents to discuss the interviews with one another and possibly provide one another with "appropriate" answers to some of the questions. Additionally, all respondents were assured that they would be guaranteed personal anonymity when findings were reported. Despite these precautions there was almost total uniformity of responses.

Consideration of why the perceptions of respondents are consistent is important because of the role these people play in the process. For example, every broker and almost every agent reported buying and restoring property in parts of the city where private urban renewal is occurring or where they believe it is imminent. Further, a number of the respondents own investment property in Georgetown, which was acquired in the past. Buying, restoring, and selling property in their own interests is conducted as an ongoing business activity apart from their regular sales activities. Brokers and real estate sales personnel are in a particularly advantageous position insofar as obtaining property is concerned. Almost all the respondents indicated that one of the major advantages to being in the business was the ability to know about good buys and to purchase houses before they were offered to the general public. This is obviously somewhat of a unique role for realtors, as they traditionally act as the liaison between someone desiring to sell a house and someone wishing to purchase a house. In the traditional real estate transaction the broker and/or salesperson is seldom the principal.

There are other interesting dimensions to real estate activities in connection with private urban renewal. An article in the *Maryland Law Review* describes the unique power position of the real estate agent as a result of the fact that very few homes are sold directly by their owners.[16] The real estate agent has access to information not directly available to the general public. They know what is available for purchase before it becomes available on the open market, since it is they who offer it for sale to the public. Additionally, they are frequently the people who appraise the property for sales purposes and tell the present owner what it would bring on the open market. Given their willingness to state that they are on the alert for good buys, and given the additional information that they are frequently the property appraisers, it is logical to assume that they are in the position to indicate to an owner that the property is worth what they personally are willing to pay to purchase it. This is particularly true of areas of private urban renewal wherein many potential sellers are absentee owners, who may have no idea of what is occurring in the immediate area. An additional advantage to their position is that, since a good part of their work time is devoted to trying to obtain and list property to sell, they also know the whereabouts of the current owner and can gauge exactly how much the latter knows about changes in a particular area.

The foregoing information provides some insight into why the respondents are so consistent in their reportage. They believe in the process they are describing. They all own property in these areas. They invest their own time and money in private urban renewal areas in an ongoing manner. It is likely that they share the same perceptions because they are actively involved in accelerating the process of private urban renewal. A self-fulfilling prophecy seems to be in operation. They indicate that they believe that a new type of community is being established and that the city is being enhanced. At the same time they are actively engaged in buying, selling, and restoring. Thus they are committed to bringing about the changes they have described.

Very few of the respondents indicated that they knew much about the history of Georgetown via direct involvement. They did, however, indicate that the process of private urban renewal there was *not* as fast as it is on Capitol Hill and in other areas of the city most recently being restored. Those who did respond tended to put the questions concerning Georgetown into a comparative context, arguing that Capitol Hill is much larger than Georgetown in area. Their statements were to the effect that Capitol Hill began to be renewed in the late 1950s. It is only twenty years later. As one respondent said, "We have restored three times the total area of Georgetown in the same time span." Another respondent stated that, "Georgetown was not at all rapid. It started with the New Deal and there are still small pockets of unrestored area there thirty years later. It is much faster on Capitol Hill and every new area of the city is likely to be faster yet."

The types of residential land-use changes that have taken place in Capitol Hill and Adams-Morgan were described as "enormous." Both these areas are perceived to have changed more during the period after 1970 than at any other time. Adams-Morgan is predicted to be the next one of these areas likely to experience rapid private urban renewal. The other two areas frequently mentioned are Dupont Circle East and Mount Pleasant. The reason for predicting rapid change in the Adams-Morgan area is that a formerly empty plot of land is being converted into an area containing at least two-hundred new townhouses. The respondents indicated that this would give Adams-Morgan an advantage that neither Georgetown nor Capitol Hill experienced. That is, a large number of middle- to upper-middle-income people are anticipated to move into these houses, changing the nature of the community. Parenthetically, most of these townhouses were sold from the "drawing board." For the most part respondents confirmed census data indicating that Adams-Morgan is in an incipient phase of private urban renewal and that the population of the area is declining rapidly. It was consistently predicted by the respondents that the next census will show dramatic population changes in all the census tracts of both Capitol Hill and Adams-Morgan.

In response to the question: "What are the overall changes in an area once it has been privately renewed?" the most immediate response is that "population declines." The reasons given for this decline are that the process of private urban renewal does two things to a neighborhood: (1) It sets off a wave of selling wherein absentee landlords sell houses that they have been renting. They sell these houses to individuals, builders, and/or contractors interested in restoring the houses. This removes a sizeable proportion of the renter population, which, in these areas, is described as poor and primarily black. The renter population, according to the reports of real estate personnel, tends to live in large family groups. As one realtor stated, "They seem to live in miscellaneous groups of up to thirty-five people." (2) As houses are restored they increase in value. This is substantiated by the sales information previously reported. As a result of increased property costs, the new buying population that replaces the renting population tends to be relatively affluent. The end result is that two people may replace ten people in a single house. The following is an account of population decrease as described by one respondent:

> In one private urban renewal block there is a house which was occupied in November of 1972 by three black families (approximately nineteen people). The house was owned by a minister of a local black church and was sold by him to a white contractor for thirteen thousand dollars in cash in December of 1972. In June, 1973, this same house was back on the market, now priced at sixty-five thousand dollars. In July of 1973 it was purchased at that sales price by a white couple, both of whom are professionally employed. In August of 1974 this house was refinanced at ninety five thousand dollars.

This is a single account, but there is reason to believe that the dynamics described are not unique. It serves to illustrate a number of residential changes. First, the population of a particular city block has been reduced; second, the value of a particular piece of urban property has increased; third, the social class position of the new members of the population is different from those who were displaced when the house was originally sold.

When queried as to why population changes in Adams-Morgan do not manifest prior to 1970, the most frequent response is that the process of private urban renewal did not take off in that area until the late 1960s. Additionally, respondents indicated that frequently when people are evicted from houses that are sold for restoration they double up with other families in the same neighborhood. As a result, the population within one house may decrease from ten to two, but the population in another house in the same census tract may increase from ten to twenty. The population within a census tract may be shifting, and more white people may be coming into the area, but they may remain a minority in the overall census tract for some time.

Realtors' Perceptions of Incoming Population

In 1967 the Capitol Hill *Prospectus* described the types of people who were moving into the area as follows: (1) young people with limited funds, most of whom are willing to do a great deal of the work themselves; (2) middle-aged people returning to the city after their children are grown—this group tends to buy already restored houses; (3) people who are subject to transfer because of job responsibilities and purchase homes with the intention of renting the property in their absence; and (4) professional restorers who move from house to house as they complete the restoration of one project after another.[17]

Realtors were questioned regarding their perceptions of the current incoming population. They were asked to describe the population in terms of race, income, occupation, and education. The types of people who are currently buying property and moving to Capitol Hill are described as young, white, childless, professionals who have joint incomes of at least thirty thousand dollars a year. They are described as being unable to afford Georgetown and tired of living in the suburbs. They are perceived to be seeking easy access to work as well as to the other facilities that the city has to offer. The people moving to the Adams-Morgan area are more frequently described as young, white, less affluent than those moving to Capitol Hill and more interested in doing a good deal of the restoration themselves.

What appears to happen, and is evidenced most clearly in the case of Georgetown, is that as the process of private urban renewal stabilizes, the price of housing inflates to the point where only the very affluent can afford to purchase in the area. To a more limited extent this has happened on Capitol Hill, where realtors indicate that one can no longer purchase a restored house for less than seventy thousand dollars. The result is that the population desiring to live in a private urban renewal area, but unable to afford one that is well underway, is likely to go off and purchase a house in an area where the process is just beginning, thus accelerating another area. Some of the respondents claimed that this has occurred recently in Capitol Hill. They state that to purchase a house that is both attractive and well-located now costs anywhere from $100,000 to $150,000. The result is that people who cannot afford to pay these prices, or will not pay these prices, look for property in Adams-Morgan, Dupont Circle East, or Mount Pleasant, where property has not inflated so rapidly. Realtors are, of course, happy to direct these people to property in other areas.

For the most part articles gathered from newspapers and other popular media sources suggest that private urban renewal is a slow, gradual process being undertaken by individual homeowners, most of whom are actively engaged in the restoration of their own houses. In an attempt to answer the question concerning the initiation and continuation of the private urban renewal phenomenon realtors were advised that this is the common view. They were asked to comment upon its accuracy in light of their knowledge of the history of private urban renewal. Most of the respondents indicated that individuals are important to the process because they are obviously the home-buying population. Without individuals to buy restored houses there is no likelihood of restoring an area. But, insofar as the role of pioneers is concerned, their responses do not substantiate the popular view of the process. Respondents indicated that pioneers have played a seminal role in calling attention to an area. However, to restore an area, more money is required that can be provided by individual homeowners. Moreover, in the early stages of private urban renewal it is difficult for individuals to obtain loans for construction or rehabilitation of property. Since a great deal of capital is required for this type of enterprise, respondents indicated that only professional builders, contractors, and speculators are in a position to spend the amounts of money required to get an entire neighborhood moving. While almost all those interviewed agreed that pioneers play a role in attracting attention to an area and help make others aware of the potential in an area, unless they are joined by realtors, contractors, builders, and speculators, it is unlikely that the area will change dramatically.

In reviewing the available data for the three areas under examination, certain demographic trends become discernible. In fact, the data and trends appear to indicate that there is a consistency that transcends time and neighborhood that may suggest the patterns in these three areas are not varied and distinct, but rather can be placed on a continuum. That is, one can view Georgetown as the first neighborhood to undergo private urban renewal in the District. In that respect it becomes a lead indicator and prototype of this phenomenon. Capitol Hill is an area that is well underway in the private urban renewal process. Some sections of this area already closely resemble Georgetown; others are still in a developmental stage. In tracing this phenomenon to the third and most recent area, Adams-Morgan, there is evidence of the emergence of this process, but only one census tract fully reflects the changes. However, there are indications that the process is underway in that neighborhood as well, although it may be in an embryonic stage of development at this time.

Notes

1. Statistics for general population trends and race were collected from the following sources: *Population and Housing Statistics for Census Tracts* (Washington, D.C.: Government Printing Office, 1942) pp. 18-22; *Census Tract*

Statistics for Washington and Adjacent Areas, Table 3 (Washington, D.C.: Government Printing Office, 1952) p. 17; *Census of Population and Housing, Final Report*, Table P-1 (Washington, D.C.: Government Printing Office, 1961), p. 16; *Census of Population and Housing, 1970, Final Report* (Washington, D.C.: Government Printing Office, 1972), p. 18.

2. See for example: Thomas F. Pettigrew, "Attitudes on Race and Housing: A Social Psychological View" in *Segregation in Residential Areas*, ed. Amos H. Hawley and Vincent P. Rock (Washington, D.C.: National Academy of Sciences, 1973), pp. 21-84; Eleanor Wolf, "The Invasion-Succession Sequences as a Self-Fulfilling Prophecy." *Journal of Social Issues* 13: (1957) 7-20.

3. Dennis E. Gale, "The Back-to-the-City Movement Revisited," Occasional Paper Series, Department of Urban and Regional Planning, George Washington University, 1977, p. 5.

4. George Grier and Eunice S. Grier, "Movers to the City" (Washington, D.C.: Washington Center for Metropolitan Studies, May 1977), p. i.

5. Statistics for median family income were collected from the following sources: *Census Tract Statistics, Washington, D.C. and Adjacent Area, Population Census Report*, Vol. III, Chapter 59 (Washington, D.C.: U.S. Department of Commerce, 1952); *United States Census of Population and Housing, Final Report 1960* (Washington, D.C.: U.S. Bureau of Commerce, 1961), pp. 16-18. *United States Census of Population and Housing*, Table P-4 (Washington, D.C.: Government Printing Office, 1972), pp. 151-161.

6. Grier and Grier, "Movers to the City," pp. i, 12, and 44.

7. Education statistics were collected from the following sources: *Population and Housing Statistics for Census Tracts*, Table 3, pp. 16-24; Table P-1, pp. 18-32, (Washington, D.C.: Government Printing Office, 1942); *United States Census of Population, General Characteristics of the Population*, Table P-1 (Washington, D.C.: United States Department of Commerce, 1952), pp. 7-11; *Census Tract Statistics*, Vol. III, Chapter 59 (Washington, D.C.: U.S. Department of Commerce, 1961), pp. 7-11; *United States Census of Population and Housing*, PHC-266 (Washington, D.C.: U.S. Department of Commerce, 1972), pp. 53-61.

8. *Washington Region, 1974, Population and Housing Data from the Washington Area Census Updating System* (Washington, D.C.: Washington Center for Metropolitan Studies, 1975), p. 9.

9. *Population and Housing Statistics for Census Tracts*, "Dwelling Units by Occupancy, Status and Race of Occupants," Table 4 (Washington, D.C.: Government Printing Office, 1942), p. 41; *United States Census of Population 1950*, "Characteristics of Dwelling Units," Vol. III, Table 3 (Washington, D.C.: Government Printing Office, 1952), pp. 32-35; *United States Census of Population and Housing*, "Occupancy and Structural Characteristics of Housing Units" (Washington, D.C.: Government Printing Office, 1961), pp. 149-158;

United Sates Census of Population and Housing, "Occupancy and Financial Characteristics of Housing Units," H-1-11 (Washington, D.C.: Government Printing Office, 1972).

10. Ibid.

11. Capitol Hill Restoration Society *Prospectus*, Fall 1960.

12. George Grier, "Private Housing Market Potential for the Central Renewal Areas of the District of Columbia" (Washington, D.C.: Washington Center for Metropolitan Studies, 1977), p. 5.

13. Gale, "The Back-to-the-City Movement Revisited," pp. 1-16.

14. See, for example: Avery M. Guest and James J. Zuiches, "Another Look at Residential Turnover in Urban Neighborhoods: A Note on Racial Change in a Stable Community by Harvey Molotch," *American Journal of Sociology* 77 (November 1971): 457-467; Harvey Molotch, "Racial Integration in a Transitional Community," *American Sociological Review* 34 (December 1969): 878-893.

15. Deirdre Stanforth and Martha Stamm, *Buying and Renovating a House in the City*, (New York: Alfred A. Knopf, 1972), p. 185.

16. "Racial Discrimination in the Private Housing Sector: Five Years After," *Maryland Law Review* 30 (1973): 308-319.

17. Capitol Hill Restoration Society *Newsletter*, Spring 1968.

5

Zoning, Preservatio and the Process of Private Urban Renew

History of Zoning

An area of important consideration in connection with private urban renewal is zoning. Zoning ordinances, which began to be passed in the 1920s, divided areas into three general types of zones. These zones are: single family; commercial; and industrial. "Blanket zoning" is the policy most frequently used to protect residential areas. It is a ranking of uses according to desirability. Single-family dwellings head the list, followed by multiple-family dwellings, apartment houses, retail, commercial, light manufacturing, and heavy industry.[1] Zoning ordinances take in far more than the distribution of municipal areas—they are concerned with and specify location, height, bulk, number of stories, size of buildings, percentage of lots which may be occupied, size of yards, courts, and other open spaces.

Zoning has been problematic and has created many conflicts of interest since its inception. According to Richard Babcock, zoning is not perceived appropriately as affecting people's lives; therefore the federal government has abstained from making any national policy decisions in this arena. However, it is clear that the singlemost function of zoning is to protect the single-family house from a variety of unpleasantries.[2]

Because the role of the federal government is not clear, most control of zoning policy has come to be a function of local government. What has emerged as a result of local control is what is known as "fiscal zoning." This is the use of zoning to achieve fiscal objectives rather than purely land-use objectives. The aim and consequence of fiscal zoning is exclusion. By employing such tactics residential areas have been able to keep out lower-income groups as well as large families, or for that matter, any groups that require public expenditures. Through the use of fiscal zoning communities are able to limit their spending on welfare, public health services, education, and other public services that would have to be paid for by the local community.

Although zoning ordinances exist in all jurisdictions of the country, the federal government exercises little authority in this matter on a local community level. The result of federal abstinence is that enormous decision-making power is left to certain groups on a local basis. Zoning can therefore be seen as the ultimate protection of the single-family community. Despite the general intent of zoning ordinances, there are occasions when the interests of the local government do not coincide with the interests of local neighborhood groups.

Additonally, there are times when the local government is not aware of these particular interests. As a result, in order to retain control over the course of development in a particular neighborhood it is necessary to gain and retain control over local zoning ordinances.

Local Zoning and Community Involvement

Two of the directives mentioned by Arthur Ziegler in his manual, *Historic Preservation of Inner City Areas* are as follows: (1) cooperate with planning and other city agencies to protect the area and to improve city services; (2) try to obtain passage of historical zoning for the area. This is very important when attempting to privately renew an urban area, because it provides the area with protection from outside forces.[3] Once an area has obtained the status of being under historical preservation, slums cannot be removed by government fiat, either by federal or local government decision. Thereafter, they must be restored from within the area on a private to semiprivate basis. The federal government will not finance the restoration of any house within an historical preserve, but it will give matching funds to community groups desiring to restore any house that has historical significance.

More important, however, is the fact that neither the local nor the federal government can tear down existing housing to make way for some type of public urban renewal, regardless of the condition of the existing housing. A neighborhood obtains autonomy in making decisions regarding needed changes in the community once it has obtained historical preservation status. The neighborhood is obligated to work cooperatively with the Fine Arts Commission in determining the fate of buildings within its boundaries. But, it prevents widespread demolition that might lead to replacement by Public Housing, or other types of public projects that the community perceives as undesirable.

Protective zoning has long been acknowledged as desirable in suburban areas. It has been used to enforce residential segregation through a variety of devices. The most common among these exclusionary tactics has been restrictions as to the type of dwelling unit permitted. This becomes very complicated as restrictions can encompass size of unit, floor space required, cost of the dwelling unit, and lot size. A combination of these factors can limit the type of population allowed to move into the community, since price can be driven up so that only the more affluent can enter an area. Interestingly enough, it is clear that local control of zoning is important to private urban renewal as well. One of the earliest sociological analyses of an attempt to gain control of local zoning by a neighborhood group is described by Walter Firey.[4] Zoning is not the central focus of Firey's study, but he perceives local control of zoning as central in the upgrading of an area. Describing the private urban renewal process in Beacon Hill, Boston, Firey discusses what residents of that area perceived to be increasing encroachments by the city at large. According to his account, threats to the integrity of the Hill finally led residents of the neighborhood to organize the Beacon Hill Association (BHA) on December 5, 1922. At this time the Boston Housing Authority was in the process of preparing new and comprehensive master zoning plans that would be applicable to the entire city. The Beacon Hill residents foresaw in this potential planning a threat to their own residential area. In response, they formed the Beacon Hill Association to have their own plans for the area incorporated into the citywide master plan. The BHA's primary interest was to restrict the building of apartment houses in the area as well as to protect old residences. Their plan was initially rejected by the city zoning board. Thereafter, a battle ensued wherein the BHA attempted to have citywide plans revised in accordance with their recommendations.

The battle was fought piece-meal over a ten-year period. The city yielded little by little to proposals put forth by the BHA. The BHA was strongly supported by influential members of the city's population, who were residents of the immediate area. Finally, what amounted to obtaining protective zoning for a particular neighborhood resulted. This allowed the community to maintain itself as a restricted residential district. This was made possible by the efforts of a well-organized community group specifically formed for these purposes.

Beacon Hill represents a reverse process—a process of private urban renewal whereby an area that was seemingly destined to become a slum was restored. The area is presently an elegant, prestigious residential neighborhood. The ability to obtain protective zoning played a considerable part in the reversal of the trend toward deterioration, and in the success of private urban renewal. Other private urban renewal areas have come to recognize the importance of zoning to their restoration. An examination of zoning issues in Georgetown and Capitol Hill makes the importance of local control clear.

Zoning Issues and the Georgetown
Community Organizations

There were two major citizens groups in Georgetown. The Georgetown Citizens Association was founded in 1924; the Georgetown Progressive Citizens Association was founded in 1926. (The Progressive Citizens Association was formed because the Georgetown Citizens Association refused to admit women. Otherwise their goals for the community were identical.) The Progressive Citizens Association deserves much credit for the private urban renewal of Georgetown.[5] The central focus of both of these groups has been zoning problems in the Georgetown area. In 1924 one of the first policy statements by a citizen group was put forth. The text of the first publication of the Georgetown Citizens Association begins by stating:

The people of Georgetown today have the opportunity to determine
its future. We may make it constantly a more and more desirable residential section or we may let it degenerate into a crowded apartment
house district. If we wish to retain its present character as a community of homes, we must secure two modifications of the zoning
regulations . . . Have you noticed what is taking place in Georgetown
today? Georgetown is on the way up. It is about to have its rebirth
as a community of homes. If Georgetown is to be made a home community the time to act is now. The zoning law can be made our safe
guard . . .[6]

The history of the private urban renewal process in Georgetown has been
closely connected to zoning issues. The initial battle for zoning changes to halt
the building of adjacent lot apartment buildings met with almost immediate
success. However, height was not restricted to three stories as the citizens
requested. The height allowance was arrived at by compromise, and a height
of five stories was accepted by the local citizens' groups in their negotiations
with the city zoning board. The groups were effective in halting the building of
newer apartment dwellings and preventing outside agencies from demolition
actions within the area.

These groups have been consistently successful over time in their efforts
to obtain protective zoning for the area. In 1933 the first comprehensive plan
for the restoration of the area was presented to the Fine Arts Commission of
the National Capitol Park and Planning Commission (currently the National
Capitol Planning Commission). The studies on which the plans were based
offered the rationale that the community should be allowed to develop its
own direction regardless of the course of the balance of the city, because it
has not always been part of the city and because consciousness of community
benefits can be generated within limited areas, whereas it is difficult to generate
citywide concerns and/or plans for redevelopment.

The process of private urban renewal in Georgetown was taking place at
approximately the same time as Beacon Hill in Boston was being renewed.
In both cases, citizens' associations were being formed in an effort to obtain
local control of neighborhood planning. In neither case did success come immediately. The dynamics of the two cases are alike in many respects. For example, the original movement to obtain protective zoning for Georgetown
began in 1926; a comprehensive plan was developed and presented to the city
government in 1933. In 1945 Georgetown was still faced with enormous problems and could still be described as having conditions that characterize slum
areas. For example, in 1948, a magazine article describes Georgetown as being a
neighborhood doing battle with rats and excess garbage, but one wherein there
is a strong preservation effort being made.[7] At this time the neighborhood was
still plagued with rats and overflowing garbage cans, and the local citizenry

saw these problems in relation to their own lack of control over zoning matters. A major portion of the problem was seen to proceed from mixed land use.

Lack of local control of zoning allowed many single-family residential houses to be used as multiple dwellings. Therefore many of the new high-income families in single-family dwellings found themselves living back-to-back with large low-income family groups. When absentee owners of these multiple dwellings were threatened with being reported for violating housing codes, their response was that they would sell the property if they were forced to reduce their tenant population. Sale of such property would threaten the historical charm of the area. If it was sold it would most likely be demolished. Demolition would provide space for construction of newer modern houses. The local associations were anxious to have the population reduced to single families in single-family dwellings, but without protective zoning they could not guarantee that the buildings, along with the population, would not be removed. Restoration of housing was perceived as desirable, as was population reduction, but replacement of housing was not what they had in mind.[8] The local citizens wanted the area upgraded, but they wanted it done in a particular fashion. Upgrading an area in accordance with certain standards requires protective zoning.

A situation similar to that described by Firey resulted. Much pressure and lobbying with the City Zoning Board took place between 1926 and 1948. In 1948 the Fine Arts Commission "placed itself and its members on record as 'heartily favoring' the amendments which were proposed as a result of community pressure."[9] This was deemed not satisfactory by the citizens. The Congressional Representative from New York, residing in Georgetown, was then requested to introduce a bill in Congress for the protection of the area. The bill is known locally as the "Old Geogetown Act." It is officially the Wadsworth Bill. The act was passed by Congress in 1950.[10] The act requires that any building constructed prior to 1851 cannot be demolished. Further, any changes or rebuilding in the area must be approved by the citizens' groups and the Fine Arts Commission. The passage of this act represented a major victory for the Georgetown citizens. Shortly thereafter these same citizens' groups requested that sixteen commercially zoned acres within Georgetown be rezoned to residential. This was immediately successful, and the rezoning was accomplished with little resistance.

Rezoning from commercial to residential appears to be agreeable to most of the residents, with the possible exception of the black population. The latter group opposed the legislation because they were afraid that the result would be an increased decline in their numbers in the immediate area. The black population was concerned because the threat of tearing down housing could no longer be used by absentee landlords. Restoration of buildings results in higher housing and rental costs. Restoration inflates the price of housing and raises taxes in an area. This makes costs prohibitive for lower-income people. With the passage of the act, the possibility of providing housing for lower-income people in the area was eliminated. The result, of course, is that the black population of Georgetown has declined dramatically over time.

In 1950 another attempt to recapture residential territory was made by the Georgetown citizens. The thrust this time was to rezone the area near the waterfront in order to ban commercial property development. After another ten-year effort, a bill was introduced and passed by Congress, placing the entire Georgetown area under the protection of the Fine Arts Commission. The result of these efforts is that Georgetown is described as the epitome of social importance in residential communities.[11]

Zoning Issues and the Capitol Hill Community

The history of Capitol Hill was described previously. The development of the area and the process of private urban renewal in the area appear to parallel that of Georgetown, although there are some problems that did not exist in Georgetown. First, there have been a number of public renewal plans for Capitol Hill over time. Georgetown was never perceived of as anything other than private urban renewal. Second, there are some objective conditions that make the two areas somewhat different. Georgetown had certainly run down over time, but it never approximated the conditions of deterioration that occurred on Capitol Hill. Part of the difference is that Georgetown had many houses that were vacant and deteriorated as a result of neglect. Capitol Hill had very few vacant dwellings until the commencement of private urban renewal. On the contrary, it has experienced overcrowded housing conditions. Private urban renewal in Georgetown began very early. It occurred at a point when the entire country was rebuilding. Capitol Hill did not exist as a residential area until after the Civil War. The major part of the construction in the area occurred in the early part of this century. Its residential population was growing as late as 1930. At the time when Georgetown was beginning its process of private urban renewal, Capitol Hill had not yet experienced its decline.

Georgetown was renewed by private efforts, partially because the country had not yet legislated for public renewal. The first public urban renewal legislation was introduced in the 1950s. Capitol Hill has had public renewal plans proposed for its rehabilitation, and there has been some public housing constructed in the area.

Since the 1950s Capitol Hill has been acknowledged as one of the nation's more serious slum problem areas. It has been depicted in many magazines and newspaper articles as a "shameful" blight on the nation's Capitol.[12]

A variety of plans have been put forth for improving the conditions that exist on Capitol Hill. For example, in 1967 the National Capitol Planning Commission (NCPC) proposed a comprehensive plan for the area, beginning their proposal with a description of the existent conditions.

> ... They include the poor conditions of a substantial amount of the housing stock; an excessive amount of land devoted to streets; incompatible mixes of housing and industry, inadequacies in schools, playspace and parks; heavy through traffic movements; traffic congestion in shopping areas; and loose, strung out arrangements of shopping facilities.[13]

One of the more important purposes of the planning proposal was to strictly enforce housing codes to protect the area from intrusion of incompatible uses. Several meetings were held with neighborhood groups, but the plan was never adopted, because, first, the NCPC was unable to reach an accord with local neighborhood groups. Second, there was no certainty that funding could be obtained even if the plan were adopted.

In 1972 another plan was put forth. This plan provided for funding by Housing and Urban Development (HUD) guaranteed low-interest loans for repairs and improvements to property. The major purpose of this plan was to bring housing up to the minimum standard required by the District of Columbia housing code. This plan was not adopted because no agreement could be reached as to who would be eligible for such loans and where the areas of concentration should be located. As a result, zoning regulations are the only existing land-use guide to planning in Capitol Hill.

Most of the Capitol Hill area is uniformly zoned. It is designed to protect the row house and the residential character of the area. Unlike Georgetown there has been a considerable amount of "spot zoning" which has allowed for commercial enterprises on corners and often in the middle of residential blocks. The area is not as thoroughly residential as Georgetown, nor is it as neatly contained. Further, Georgetown began to attempt to obtain control of local zoning before much "spot zoning" had been allowed. Capitol Hill is in the position of having to reverse an already existing encroachment on its residential character. An additional problem is that, since most of the building is post-Civil War, the area is not of as much historical importance as is the Georgetown area.

The Capitol Hill Restoration Society (CHRS) was founded in 1955 for the purpose of encouraging restoration in the area. In the early 1960s there were two hundred members; in 1970 there were twelve hundred members; in 1976 there were close to two thousand members. In 1973 another large citizens' group was formed in the Capitol Hill area. It grew out of a number of splinter groups who are opposed to the policies of the Capitol Hill Restoration Society. This latter group is the Capitol East Housing Coalition (CEHC). It is affiliated with the Capitol East Community Organization described in a previous chapter.

The purpose of forming CEHC is to help keep low- and moderate-income families in the area. They perceive the purposes of the CHRS to be in direct opposition to their goals. As a result, Capitol Hill had two large, active community groups. Unlike the case in Georgetown, these two groups were not in accord and did not share the same goals for the area.

Part of the difficulty in obtaining historical preservation status for the Capitol Hill area is a direct result of the conflict of interests between these two groups and the respective populations that they represent. The CHRS recognizes the advantages of obtaining historical protection and believes this status is necessary for successful private urban renewal. The CEHC recognizes the dangers to the poor and to the renting population if this type of protection is obtained. Their argument is that it will aid Capitol Hill in becoming a replication of Georgetown. Recall that in 1930 most of the blacks who lived in Georgetown were tenants. This is true of Capitol Hill as well, although about 25 percent of this population was homeowners in 1970. CEHC is concerned that both black renter and owner populations will be forced out if private urban renewal continues.[14] Moreover, they fear that local control of zoning will ultimately mean white, middle-class control of zoning.

The struggle for local control of zoning in Capitol Hill has not been a simple procedure, although the CHRS has gained strength over time. For example, in 1959 150 units of new apartment buildings were constructed in the area despite their protests. Since 1964, with the accelerated process of private urban renewal underway, they have achieved some major victories. In June of 1964 Congress attempted to pass legislation that would allow two or more blocks of the Capitol Hill area to be removed to make way for a parking garage. The organized efforts of the CHRS blocked the appropriation of funds for this action. Moreover, they successfully argued that building for Congress should, in the future, be aimed toward the Mall and not to the East. It is possible for the issue to be reopened, but at the moment it has been halted.[15]

One of the splinter groups that ultimately merged into the CEHC was called Success Incorporated. In 1969 the CHRS and Success Incorporated engaged in a struggle over the rezoning of an empty school building in one of the more completely restored areas of Capitol Hill. Success Incorporated wanted the building rezoned on a "spot zoning" basis to use it as a community center. They argued that such "spot zoning" was not inconsistent with the history of zoning on Capitol Hill. The CHRS argued that putting a community center in a restored area was inappropriate. They claimed that such construction should be prevented because such an entity in a restored area would amount to an anomaly. The issue of the community center was argued before the District Zoning Commission. The arguments of the CHRS were upheld, and the building still stands empty. More important, the CHRS took this single issue and parlayed it into a more general policy. Since that time they have been in the forefront of any proposed zoning changes on Capitol Hill. In 1971 they proposed a plan whereby all "spot zoning" would be halted in the Capitol Hill area. This proposal was agreed to by the District Zoning Commission.[16] What is interesting about this gradual taking of control over zoning decisions by the CHRS is that while both planners and citizen groups may make proposals concerning zoning, the only decision-making power resides in the legislative body or with the city council. The CHRS, however, has managed to obtain advisory status with the Zoning Commission and requests for zoning changes on Capitol Hill must be reviewed and voted on by their membership before they are presented to the District Zoning Commission. Thus, although they have not yet managed to gain complete local control over zoning issues, they are now in a position to screen requests for changes.

One of the major areas of conflict between the CHRS and the CEHC concerns the question of "concentrated code enforcement." This means that certain selected areas would be subjected to strict housing code enforcement. The areas that would be affected have not been specified, but the CEHC is vigorously opposed to the passage of such legislation. Their belief is that it will most affect black homeowners, who will be unable to afford to remedy the violations and will have to sell their property. The CHRS is a supporter of this proposal, and since 1967 it has been encouraging the District government to implement such a plan in the Capitol Hill area.[17]

The CHRS has compiled an inventory of sites and buildings of historical value in the area. The purpose of compiling such an inventory is to designate boundaries for a Capitol Hill Historical District. An effort is being made to include as much of the Capitol Hill area as possible within the protected area.

The first steps in attaining historical preservation status have been accomplished. Capitol Hill, largely through the efforts of the CHRS, has been placed in Category II of the District of Columbia's Inventory of Historic Sites. It has been recommended as eligible for nomination to the National Register of Historic Places. Because it is in a position pending approval and not yet a historic place, the area is only partially protected. In the meantime it cannot be assigned any additional public housing. The city and the federal governments cannot approve any demolition permits without a 180-day interval wherein citizens have the opportunity to argue against the changes.[18] If the area is placed on the National Register, it will be safe from outside interference and can then develop its own internal zoning codes in much the same manner as Georgetown.

Zoning Issues and the Adams-Morgan Community

Adams-Morgan is primarily zoned R-4, which is a residential classification equivalent to that of Capitol Hill. The second largest category of housing in the area is apartment buildings (R 5-B). According to District standards many of these apartment buildings are overcrowded. This area of the city houses the largest Spanish surnamed population in the District. Presently the most articulate group in the community is AMO, whose purpose is to retain its current racial and economic homogeneity.

The private urban renewal process in Adams-Morgan is in an embryonic stage. The major changes in the area are occurring in condominium conversion of apartment buildings, although there is a considerable amount of new construction as well. For example, 218 townhouses were constructed between 1977 and 1978. These houses were originally planned to sell for between $60,000 and $80,000. Resales are already up to $100,000. This construction has had an impact on the surrounding areas as two entire city blocks of townhouses in the immediate vicinity have recently sold for restoration, and packages of houses on other blocks are currently being purchased for the same purpose.

Thus far there is no counterpart of the Georgetown Citizen's Association or the Capitol Hill Restoration Society in Adams-Morgan. However, there are many old buildings in the area that are of historical interest. Adams-Morgan has experienced as much spot zoning as had Capitol Hill, and the result is a residential area interspersed with commercial establishments. In 1975, for the first time, one of the local newspapers of the community expressed the "growing concern" about spot zoning in the area.[19] If the private urban renewal process proceeds, and there is every indication that it will do so, it is possible that a prorestoration force will emerge. It is likely to occur when enough residents believe that they must protect their immediate environment both from encroachments by the city government and from elements within the community that are not desirable. Private urban renewal had its very beginning in Georgetown in the early 1920s. In the mid-1920s its citizen groups were formed, and their zoning struggles have continued into the 1960s. Restoration of Capitol Hill began in 1950. The Restoration Society was not founded until 1955 and in the early 1960s had only two hundred members. It apparently takes some time into the private urban renewal process before a community is convinced of the direction it wants to take. It is understandable that Adams-Morgan is yet to develop such a preservation group.

Obtaining Historical Preservation status for a particular area, and gaining local control over zoning decisions are not synonomous. In the first case certain objective criteria must be met. These criteria vary from city to city, because original construction dates back to different periods. Thus, Williamsburg in Virginia, Georgetown in the District of Columbia, and Old Town in Virginia date back to Colonial America. In other cities such as Toledo, Ohio, the oldest architecture may date only to the turn of the century. Historical Preservation status is flexible and can be applied to different historical epochs as appropriate. Historical Preservation entails public funds for a number of different enterprises. For example, the Historical Preservation Act of 1966 authorizes federal grants to states on a matching basis for the purpose of conducting architectural surveys to delineate potential areas. Thereafter, obtaining funds for actual restoration of housing can be obtained through local and federal agencies, although these funds are available with numerous qualifications regarding both the physical premises and the ultimate population composition of the given area. For instance, existing buildings within the specified boundaries must remain unchanged on the exterior. The original facade must remain intact. Moreover, guidelines for interior rehabilitation are sometimes severely limited as well. Various federal subsidies are available for rehabilitation, but they are few in number and hardly generous in allocation and are usually limited to low- and moderate-income residents.

Historical Preservation status is most often sought for an area after private urban renewal is well underway. Moreover, it usually comes about as a result of some external threat to the buildings within a given community. In most cases a historical building is slated for demolition by a government agency or a private corporation. When the local community learns of such a potential plan, it frequently organizes to halt the proposed destruction. They may or may not be successful in their initial efforts. But, thereafter the community musters its forces to prevent additional externally imposed change from occurring.

Obtaining local control of zoning decisions is a different type of phenomenon. Historically most decisions regarding housing have been made in the private sector. The nature of the free enterprise system dictates that the housing industry remain relatively free of governmental direction and control. Local zoning boards decree the direction of specific areas; they are appointed by the elected officials, and for the most part their decisions are absolute. In urban areas local zoning boards frequently are advised by those who have the most financial interest and investment in an area. In many cases this is the real estate industry along with practicing attorneys, aided by city planners and local legislators. Frequently citizens are unaware of zoning policy and/or particular decision-making processes. This is especially true in urban areas because of the widely varied land use that exists. It is only when zoning decisions begin to affect particular areas that citizens groups become active.

In the private urban renewal areas these dynamics are particularly interesting. In the early stages of private urban renewal there is little local control of zoning. As areas improve it becomes clear that this control is necessary if a residential area is to be developed. Local groups, initially aided by realtors, form to impose their wishes on the local zoning board. As the private urban renewal process continues, and the residential character of the community becomes increasingly protected conflicts, emerge. Realtors, who initially were in accord with and supportive of community organizations find themselves at variance with these groups. What transpires is that it is initially in the realtors' interest to support the development of a residential area. Later it is to their advantage to attempt to introduce both apartment buildings and commercial establishments into the area. At this point they find themselves arguing with their former allies, who are still dedicated to retaining and protecting single-family housing. The realtors, who at first favored local control of zoning, may find themselves arguing before the community groups for zoning changes. Moreover, they may find themselves opposed to obtaining Historical Preservation status for an area because it severely limits their financial operations. Once the private urban renewal process is well underway, those who initially were among its strongest supporters find themselves handicapped by the very process that they aided in accelerating. Moreover, they often find themselves in the position of losing zoning arguments with local community groups as the latter gain in strength and increasingly take control of decision-making within these areas. Three recent cases in the District illustrate this conflict. Two of these conflicts have taken place on Capitol Hill. In the first conflict, a long established realtor and strong supporter of the Restoration Society requested permission to construct an office and/or apartment building on a large tract of vacant land in his possession. The Restoration Society refused his request arguing that the low density character of the neighborhood as well as the historic quality would be detrimentally effected if this building were permitted. As a result the Restoration Society has refused to consider his request for a necessary zoning change, and the realtor was forced to take the case into court. The court decision upheld the view of the Restoration Society. A second case concerned a long-time builder and contractor and a local owner who planned to demolish a row of houses to make room for the construction of new town houses. The owner and the contractor had agreed to undertake this project as a joint venture. Because these buildings are located in an historic district permission is required to alter the facade or to demolish property. The Restoration Society cannot grant permission nor can it refuse permission, but it can refuse to recommend the requested changes and possibly tie the property into litigation for an indefinite period of time. In this case a compromise was achieved wherein the Society agreed to allow the demolition of some of the buildings if the balance were retained in their original historic condition.

Another illustration is offered in Georgetown. For many years the citizens groups have been attempting to downgrade commercial property along the waterfront to residential zoning. The realtors and builders who originally supported the citizens' efforts to restore Georgetown have been engaged in a struggle to retain the commercial status of this property. The realtors and builders have argued that the property is peripheral to the residential area, since it borders the waterfront and historically has been used for commercial purposes. The citizens groups have argued that Georgetown has enough commercial development and that the area does not need to increase its density. After many years of litigation the court has ruled in favor of the builders.

Notes

1. Ronald E. Grieson, *Urban Economics* (Boston: Little, Brown, 1973), p. 135.

2. Richard F. Babcock, *The Zoning Game* (Madison, Wisc.: University of Wisconsin Press, 1969).

3. Arthur P. Ziegler, Jr., *Historic Preservation in Inner City Areas* (Pittsburgh: Allegheny Press, 1971), p. 14.

4. Walter Firey, *Land Use in Central Boston* (Cambridge, Mass.: Harvard University Press, 1947).

5. Colin Cochrane, "The Georgetown Story," *National Capitol Area Realtor*, March 1959.

6. Alvin M. West, *The Future of Georgetown*, Georgetown Peabody Collection (May 1924), pp. 3-4.

7. *Saturday Evening Post*, 20 March 1948.

8. "Notes on Georgetown," *Georgetown Portfolio*, Washingtonian Room, Martin Luther King Library.

9. *Journal of the American Society of Architectural Historians*, 8 (October 1948): 14-17.

10. "Notes on Georgetown," *Georgetown Portfolio*.

11. This description appeared in an article describing charming communities in the United States that are well worth visiting. *Holiday Magazine*, February 1950.

12. *Evening Star*, 17 September 1949.

13. National Capitol Planning Commission, *Position Paper*, Spring 1967.

14. See for example: Susan Jacoby, "Capitol Hill Integration Masks Conflicts," *New Republic*, January 1969.

15. *Washington Post*, 25 April 1975.

16. Capitol Hill Restoration Society, *Newsletter*, March 1971.

17. Capitol Hill, *Gazette*, 11 November 1967.

18. National Trust for Historic Preservation, Washington, D.C.

19. The *In Towner* 112 (December 1975).

6

Political and Social Consequences of Private Urban Renewal

Displacement: National Analysis

There has been little sociological examination of private urban renewal. This neglect probably has to do with the nature of the process itself. That is, the dominant population migration pattern in the United States is still one in which a white population is moving to the suburbs. However, there are indicators that this trend has slowed down.[1] In addition, there is now evidence of black migration to the suburbs as well.[2] Something new is happening in U.S. residential patterns, and there is strong evidence that white middle-class people are purchasing homes and moving into certain areas of the central cities. It is difficult to describe these population shifts with complete accuracy at this time. It is likely that when 1980 census data are available these patterns of change will emerge more dramatically.

Part of the reason for sociological neglect of the private urban renewal process is that, thus far, it has not had serious impact on cities. For example, Georgetown now represents elegant inner city living and Capitol Hill comes close to replicating those conditions. Moreover, there are other such residential areas in cities across the country. Brooklyn Heights and Cobble Hill in New York; Seton Hill and Bolton Hill in Baltimore; Society Hill and Germantown in Philadelphia; Beacon Hill and the South End of Boston all qualify as such areas. But the changes brought about by the process of private urban renewal have not been experienced on a citywide level. From 1950 to 1975 the black population of many cities continuously increased. Residential segregation patterns in most cities have been maintained; cities have experienced a series of "civil disturbances"; public facilities and services have continued to decay. The overall pattern of urban deterioration has not been halted, although there is evidence of dramatic reversal in private urban renewal areas. The end result is that while cities as a whole may not be registering the positive benefits of private urban renewal, the negative effects of the process are visible. The most serious negative consequence of private urban renewal is displacement. The question is whether or not the process will grow, gathering enough momentum to reverse the downward spiral into which inner cities have fallen. And, will the end result be revitalized heterogeneous communities of mixed age, income and race, or will a new type of homogeneous residential setting result?[3]

Thus far it appears likely that the latter pattern will dominate. Consequently it is frequently claimed that displacement looms as a major problem for the next decade. Yet, displacement is not new, nor is it necessarily linked to private urban renewal. In fact, the most extensive displacement has occurred as a result of public urban renewal projects. Two dominant patterns of displacement have been engaged in by federal and local governments. Private urban renewal is perhaps a third variation on the theme. The first type of displacement occurs when an area is declared a slum in need of clearance. Replacement in this case is with buildings intended for higher-income tenants. Although the slumlike conditions are often cited as the reason for redevelopment of the area, it is no accident that the areas are well located and convenient for those who work in the city. This type of displacement is well-documented.[4] A second type of displacement occurs when slum areas are cleared and replaced with low-income public housing. In this case we often construct concentrations of poor populations in newer housing, accommodating far less of the population than had originally lived in the area.[5] These are patterns of displacement that involve large numbers of people. There are, of course, other ways in which people are displaced. Industrial shifts, manufacturing plant and military base relocation also displace people in large numbers. Upper echelon personnel often move along with the work site, but lower level personnel are left behind to seek other employment in the area or are forced to move to other areas to seek employment. Some have argued that rent control laws contribute to displacement because they put in motion a cycle wherein landlords argue that they cannot afford to maintain the buildings unless rents are raised accordingly.[6] As a result buildings slide into disrepair and are ultimately abandoned. The South Bronx section of New York City is illustrative of displacement due to fires. As buildings burn down they are abandoned, and people are forced to move elsewhere. The point is that displacement has many causes.

Private urban renewal may very well be the least important of these patterns of displacement. Reports from major cities indicate that people are being removed in the wake of private urban renewal. Displacement as a result of this process is reported to be a political issue in Atlanta, Georgia; Baltimore, Maryland; Boston, Massachusetts; and Hartford, Connecticut to cite a few such locales.[7] Although data are not reliable after 1970, there is enough evidence to suggest that the private urban renewal process is making an impact. For example, Black states that it is common to most large cities, but that it is small in relation to the overall city. However, he goes on to argue that the amount is growing and anticipated to continue.[8] In 1976, the *Wall Street Journal* reported that the preservation movement is growing and gathering strength and that it may ultimately encompass large areas of entire cities.[9] Realtors indicate that there is increased interest in older city housing.[10] Circulation of *Old House Journal*, written to give advice concerning renovation of older homes, has doubled in a very short period.[11] Builders have suggested that in order for people to be able to afford to purchase homes the city must be recycled.

Their argument is that costs of suburban building are becoming prohibitive to middle-class Americans.[12]

Nationwide reports indicate that renter populations are the most likely to be evicted during the process of private urban renewal.[13] It is quite possible that displacement occurs in direct proportion to the number of houses purchased for restoration. However, the extent of the displacement phenomenon is an empirical question. We have not known in the past how many people were displaced by renewal projects nor where they went after removal. The same is true of displacement accompanying private urban renewal. Despite the concern expressed by public offices and local community groups, no one is certain as to the numbers entailed in the displacement nor is there any way of determining where people are going. Part of the difficulty lies in obtaining data and devising a method by which to measure displacement. Census data are collected at too infrequent intervals to allow for precise measure. Given an interval of ten years, it is too late to do anything except determine how many people have gone from an area. It is not possible to determine when in the ten-year interval most of the movement took place nor is it possible to determine where the displaced have gone. To measure the displacement impact of private urban renewal on a national level it is essential to devise a new method of population recording that would signal that an area is in the process of change, allowing adequate time to determine what is occurring before the population is removed. An indepth discussion of displacement on a national level is beyond the scope of this book. It is possible, however, to examine closely the process in limited areas.

Displacement: Nation's Capital

As mentioned in the discussion of Georgetown, one of the motivating forces in the restoration of that area was the severe housing shortage in the District. The vacancy rate in the District is currently less than 3 percent, indicating that the city is again experiencing a severe housing shortage. The vacancy rate citywide is obtained by including only "livable" units; the count does not include government-owned housing or housing that is boarded up or housing that is currently included under "pending planning decisions." The latter type of housing is city owned as well, but no decision has been made as to its future use. The volume of vacant privately owned housing units in the city has been steadily declining since 1970. These shortages are particularly evident in Adams-Morgan, Dupont Circle, and the fringe areas of Capitol Hill.[14] As of 1974, there was a waiting list for District public housing of about 7,000 families. However, at this time, the only new public housing being constructed in the District is for the elderly. Since the federal moratoria imposed in the early

1970s housing construction for low- and moderate-income households has been virtually halted.

Some parallels between the occurrence of private urban renewal and a citywide housing scarcity are being repeated. The renewal of Georgetown was accompanied by a sharp decrease in renter population during a time of housing scarcity. This time the decrease in renter population is occurring in other areas of the city, most particularly Capitol Hill. There is no evidence to suggest that the process of private urban renewal creates housing shortages. However, the shortages are of concern to groups involved with providing services to lower-income populations. The crux of the problem is that in areas where the process of private urban renewal is occurring, the renter population, frequently large at the outset, is the most rapidly displaced. The process aggravates the housing shortage rate, because many "livable" houses are left standing empty for long periods while they undergo restoration. Frequently after the restoration is completed most of the displaced population can no longer afford to rent in the area, even if the housing is not planned exclusively for owner occupancy. Another factor is that it is believed that the process of private urban renewal, wherever it is occurring, is displacing populations in numbers too great to be accommodated elsewhere. In the District the population being displaced is black, poor, and powerless. Moreover, there is no way currently available for the city government to assist these people in relocation.[15] Again, whereas there is no way to offer absolute numbers, there are enough illustrations to make the situation clear. For example, in the summer of 1973, an entire block of houses three blocks from the U.S. Capitol was sold by one owner to nineteen individual homeowners. These buildings were six-bedroom houses being utilized as rooming houses. They were then converted into single-family dwellings.[16] In the fall of 1973 eviction notices were sent out on eleven properties in the Adams-Morgan area. Several of the families moved on receipt of these notices. Others, in conjunction with a local community group, decided to fight the eviction notices in court. A spokesman for the group urged the owner not to sell to whites and further stated in a street rally press conference: "We're here today to make clear to the rest of the real estate vultures and land speculators that we will not sit back and watch our community be sold out from beneath us like Georgetown, Southwest and Capitol Hill." Subsequently, the owner of the property decided not to pursue the eviction and remodel the premises on this street. Rather, he sold the houses to individual investors and developers. Looking back at this one block where houses sold in the $7,000 to $15,000 range in 1973, one finds these same houses selling for well over $100,000 in 1978.[17] Another transaction in Adams-Morgan illustrates much the same dynamics. A row of houses on one particular block were sold fully tenanted and unremodeled for $26,000 per house. These houses were sold only weeks later for $65,000 per house. Remodelers are now working on these houses and sales prices are expected to be in excess of $125,000.[18]

There are those who argue that the private urban renewal process promises new life for the inner cities. If it is successful it will increase the city tax base, improve city services, rehabilitate deteriorating neighborhoods, and reverse the process of decay that has occurred in many of the central cities of the United States. There are, however, those who perceive this process to be a threat. The nature of the conflict concerning this process is one wherein builders, realtors, contractors, and speculators are interested in accelerating the process of private urban renewal. The process is perceived as a threat by the renter population of the areas where it is occurring. Over time it becomes a threat to the original homeowning population as well because of rising tax assessments as surrounding property and housing is improved. In the District of Columbia the conflict has accelerated and has involved a number of conflicting interest groups on either side of the issue. It has also engaged the attention of the city government. The dynamics of the conflict and the roles played by some of the participants are discussed next.

Participants in the Conflict

On June 8, 1974, a conference was held under the title of "Blockbusting—1974 Style." The focus of this conference was to discuss what is currently being referred to as reverse blockbusting; a process in which a white, middle-class population is invading certain urban neighborhoods that have formerly been both black and primarily poor in population composition.

The conference was organized by the Capitol East Community Organization (CECO), a local group committed to halting the process of private urban renewal and preserving the rights of the renters in the community. They were joined in their organizing efforts by the Adams-Morgan Community Organization (AMO), a local community organization in another area of the city committed to the same goals. Representatives of the local Board of Realtors, members of the newspaper associations, and a few academics were included on the panels. The manifest purpose of the conference was to discuss ways and means to halt the process of private urban renewal primarily in Capitol Hill and Adams-Morgan, but peripherally in Mount Pleasant and Dupont Circle East as well.

The conference centered on a discussion of the advantages and disadvantages of heterogeneous housing patterns. The key-note address began with a discussion of reverse blockbusting. The first question raised was, "What is unscrupulous about blockbusting?" The speaker stressed that this practice could not be fairly evaluated in isolation. Rather, it has to be analyzed in the context of general housing patterns in the United States.

Urban social theory leads one to the conclusion that people prefer to live in stable, homogeneous communities. If people are moving into areas that are not homogeneous, particularly if a higher status group is invading a lower status group's area, they must have some reason for assuming that the area will become homogeneous over time. This is clear in the reports from interviews with realtors, almost all of whom predict that the process of private urban renewal will ultimately result in better living conditions, less density of population, and sound financial investment. Whether their perceptions of reality are accurate or not is irrelevant. To the extent that they believe this is the case, it is more than likely that what they perceive to be true will ultimately be true in its consequences. This is what is concerning groups such as CECO and AMO. As they watch the communities increasingly change as private urban renewal continues, they are witnessing a self-fulfilling prophecy in action.

If a white, middle-class group is invading an area that is poor and primarily black, it must hold the belief that change is imminent. Otherwise, the financial risk is too great. The nature of the conflict between CECO and AMO and the people involved in private urban renewal is in many respects a conflict of economics. The populations represented by the two local organizations are the poor, renting groups. The invading population is affluent, well-educated and economically dominant.

To put the conflict exclusively into an economic perspective is to simplify the dynamics somewhat. Many historical forces combine to promote the homogeneity of local areas. According to one realtor, the Federal Housing Authority would not guarantee loans to the inner city in private urban renewal areas prior to 1958. As a result of this policy, many lower-income people were unable to purchase property because of the requirements of high down-payments with conventional mortgages. At the present time, the Federal Housing Authority is willing to guarantee almost any mortgage. But this change in policy position did not transpire until private urban renewal was already well underway. By that time the prices of housing were so inflated that lower-income people were no longer eligible to apply for such mortgages.

The situation is one in which there is a conflict of interests between those who are in favor of heterogeneous neighborhoods and those who are involved in the process of private urban renewal. The people who want to make a profit aid the latter group.

Role of Local Government in the Conflict

As an outgrowth of the efforts of the groups involved in the conference on "Blockbusting—1974 Style," two of the District of Columbia Council members were approached by the groups who oppose private urban renewal. Incidentally, or coincidentally, the two City Council people who were approached represent Capitol Hill and Adams-Morgan, and both are in danger of losing their respective constituencies as a result of the population changes occurring in these areas.

After much lobbying with the City Council, on April 1, 1975, a bill was introduced and referred to the Committee on Finance and Revenue. The bill is called
the "Real Estate Transaction Tax of 1975."[19] It has come to be popularly
referred to as the "Speculator Bill." The broad purpose of the bill is to limit
tenant evictions for the purpose of rehabilitation; to limit speculation, and
subsequently to halt price inflation in the city.

The specific purpose of the bill is as follows: "The proposed Real Estate
Transaction Tax Act is designed to deter the speculative buying and selling of
homes within the District." As written, the bill would impose a substantial
tax on certain kinds of deeds, which are recorded in connection with the sales
transactions of a house. The bill pertains to houses that have been sold more
than once within a certain time period. Therefore the shorter the time a house
is owned the higher the tax. Taxes are based on profit. For example, if a property is sold after an ownership period of up to eight months and the profit is
49 percent upon resale, 50 percent of that profit would be taxed. The legislation applies only to residential row houses.

The first public hearing on the tax took place on June 19, 1975.[20] The
hearing erupted in anger at many points. The proponents of the bill arrived,
accompanied by a number of evicted tenants, and acted out some guerrilla
theatre vignettes. The opponents of the bill made sarcastic comments about
"socialism in our time," as well as a number of speeches about the "sanctity
of private property rights in America." Overall the hearing resulted in chaos,
and one District Council member stated, "no one said anything that we haven't
all heard before."

The second public hearing regarding this bill was held on November 25,
1975,[21] and resulted in much the same type of insult exchange and anger as
more suggestions were added to the proposed legislation. Immediately after
this hearing the Washington Residential Development Coalition (WRDC) was
formed to fight the passage of the bill. The WRDC is broadbased and represents almost all facets of the real estate industry in the area. The purpose of
the formation of the WRDC is that, "The fight against the transaction tax must
be waged now with the utmost intensity so that the abolition, not the revision
of a 'speculation tax' concept may be achieved."[22]

The third public hearing was held on December 9, 1975. By this time the
WRDC was organized. They had circulated letters to homeowners in the District
of Columbia, particularly in the private urban renewal areas, urging them to
oppose the proposed legislation. They had urged that all individual homeowners
attend the public hearings to argue that: (1) the proposed legislation will slow
down private urban renewal because investors will not be willing to pay these
taxes. As a result they will take their efforts elsewhere, leaving the city to continued deterioration. If this occurs, those who were willing to invest in private
urban renewal will find that the areas will not improve over time. And (2) the
proposed legislation is not revenue productive because it will affect any number

of subsidiary agencies who have been employed by those who are actively engaged in private urban renewal, such as plumbing firms, electric firms, heating and air conditioning firms. As a result, the unemployment rate in the city may rise dramatically if private urban renewal is halted.

The WRDC avoided the topic of speculation entirely, focusing the bulk of their arguments in other directions. By this time they were in a position to offer a counter-proposal, which they argued would aid in offsetting the basic problem, lack of available housing for the poor.

One of the techniques used by real estate boards is discussed in an article by Donald Bouma. He claims that frequently when they want something stopped they simply say that they have a better idea.[23] Then they initiate their own plan and begin to argue around it as though it was always the central issue. What Bouma describes is exactly what the WRDC is attempting to do in their negotiations concerning the pending legislation. They have proposed a counter-plan for providing housing for the people who are being evicted from areas undergoing private renewal. They have hired a professional group to discredit the recommendations upon which the potential bill was based. The discrediting study was conducted by the Homer Hoyt Institute, pursuant to a grant from the WRDC. This research group evaluated the methods and conclusions of the study on which the bill is based. They not only contradicted the findings of the report and criticized the methodology used to write it, but also reversed the nature of the underlying issue. The Homer Hoyt Institute stated: "The analysis asserts, without evidence, that 'speculation' is contributing to the rise in housing prices, when in fact it is the rise in housing prices that is giving someone a speculative profit."[24]

For the next meeting the battle arena was moved. After a series of public hearings that did not go particularly well for the WRDC, the meeting place was relocated to a more private facility where the realtors could discuss the consequences of the legislation. This meeting took place at a local hotel on March 25, 1976. It is interesting that the speaker for the evening was the chairman of the District of Columbia City Council. The cost of attendance was $14.50. It is unlikely that many members of the opposition attended this meeting, and it is most unlikely that any evicted tenants were in attendance.

After the 1976 meeting the bill disappeared from public view for awhile and emerged again as D.C. Law 2-91 effective July 30, 1978. As this legislation passed through committee it was revised and watered down considerably. Not only was it delayed for more than two years, but the following illustration will indicate its fate. A builder buys a property for $50,000 and remodels it for an additional $50,000 and sells it for a total price, within six months of his initial purchase, of $160,000. The profit of $60,000 would be taxed at the level of 90 percent. Thus the profit to the builder is only $6,000 and the city picks up a profit (tax) of $54,000. Under this disincentive, very few developers would bother going through the acquisition, eviction, financing, restoration, and sales stages to earn such a pittance. Thus tenants would presumably remain secure in their rental units.

However, as the "speculator tax" finally evolved from the City Council the entire displacement issue was either lost or avoided. Under the revised bill passed as Law 2-91 in the summer of 1978, the builder would merely warrantee the basic heating, electrical, and plumbing systems on his newly remodeled house and thus would be entirely exempt from this tax. One vocal council member called this gaping loophole "one of the biggest sellouts to the real estate industry ever seen."

The conflict concerning private urban renewal and the resultant legislation is interesting in light of information regarding community organization. It is clear that when individuals perceive that they are being pushed too far they do organize to protect their own interests. However, in much the same sense in which it is too late to worry about displacement once it has occurred, it may be too late to organize to halt a process once it is well underway. For example, there is very little talk about halting private urban renewal in Capitol Hill. The restoration of this area appears to be regarded as a *fait accompli.* The active community groups opposed to the process of private urban renewal in Capitol Hill have virtually disappeared. The area of conflict has shifted to newly restored areas of the city such as Adams-Morgan. Moreover, the outcome of the legislative battle is a puzzlement. On the one hand it might be stated that local community groups have been victorious because legislation imposing high taxes on speculation has been passed. On the other hand, one might wonder what conceivable effect this legislation can have on displacement. As far as can be determined, the speculators are not the group responsible for displacing people. They are quite content to buy and sell property with or without tenants as the case may be. It is the builders who have to evict tenants to restore buildings for resale. What the legislation has created is a situation wherein builders are tax exempt. Additionally, it may encourage those who formerly confined their activities to speculation to become builders thus accelerating the process even further. The unintended consequences may produce the exact opposite of what was originally intended; the bill may accelerate rather than slow down displacement. Murray Stedman states:

> The realtor and his colleagues play an essential part in upgrading, downgrading or maintaining the status quo of a community. Legally recognized as private entrepreneurs, the real estate brokers—working closely with the zoning boards and allied interests—have become an important element in social control. They can determine—all other things being equal—the social composition of a community . . . Taken together, it could be argued that the contractors, the builders, the unions, the realtors, and the zoning officials constitute a system of private government. Using such criteria as income, ethnicity, and religion, they rather effectively determine housing patterns and allocate housing for most Americans.[25]

His contention is supported by Leonard Downie who argues: ". . . it is usually the real estate industry that determines whether destruction by 'renewal' or revival through 'unslumming' will take place, depending upon which it finds more profitable."[26]

Thus far there is reason to accept these contentions in the District of Columbia. The District of Columbia is not unique in this respect. If there is a "system of private government" that determines housing patterns in the United States, this private system can only exist because there is a vacuum in official government policy as it relates to housing. There are three major federal housing programs: urban renewal, established in 1949 with the express purpose of aiding urban areas by clearing slums; subsidized low-income public housing, which was initiated in 1937; and mortgage insurance programs administered through the Federal Housing Authority and the Veteran's Administration. The first two of these housing programs are directed primarily at urban areas; the latter has aided in suburban expansion. Two more recently introduced programs are Model Cities and Urban Homesteading. Both of these programs are directed toward inner city rehabilitation. The first of these requires that a comprehensive plan for inner city renewal be submitted, as well as local financial contributions. This plan goes beyond housing per se. It can include social programs such as health care, education, and plans for combatting poverty. Urban Homesteading is an effort to solve the housing abandonment problem. The theory is that individuals who are willing to restore and live in abandoned housing should be given economic incentives to encourage them in this endeavor. Costs to cities are low, and individuals are expected to pay a nominal fee with the stipulation that they will restore the housing and live in the area.

Because there is no dearth of available federal housing programs, we must raise the question as to why there is a vacuum that allows private interests to direct housing policy. It is possible to isolate a major area of difficulty contributing to the existence of this vacuum. This difficulty lies in the nature of multileveled government, which makes program implementation more than a little difficult.

Multiple layers of government are obviously accompanied by multiple layers of bureaucratic procedure, replication, and inefficiency at the very least. To illustrate this difficulty one need only point out the complexity entailed in such structures. More than 70 percent of the U.S. population lives in metropolitan areas.[27] Standard Metropolitan Statistical Areas, as defined by the U.S. Bureau of the Census involve two considerations:

> . . . first, a city or cities of specified population to constitute the central city and to identify the county in which it is located as the central county, and, second, economic and social relationships with contiguous counties which are metropolitan in character, so that the periphery of the specific metropolitan area may be determined.[28]

Practically defined, a metropolitan area consists of a city and its surrounding suburbs. Utilizing this definition, metropolitan New York consists of twenty-two counties, nine in New Jersey, twelve in New York, and one in Connecticut. There are at least fourteen hundred distinct political units within this one metropolitan area. The metropolitan area of Washington, District of Columbia, includes three independent cities, and seven closely located counties; it extends into two adjoining states, Maryland and Virginia. In 1967 twenty-four Standard Metropolitan Statistical Areas with populations greater than one million had a combined total of 20,703 units of government.[29] Moreover, all these units of government operate simultaneously with frequently overlapping spheres of jurisdiction.

Evaluation of all the federal housing programs is not possible within the confines of this book. However, when attempting to assess these programs this multilayered governmental structure must be taken into account. For example, urban renewal has aided in the physical rehabilitation of inner cities. However, the result of such programs has been to raise the cost of housing such that the population eligible to live in these areas is limited to the middle-income group. In addition, it has reduced the available quantity of inner city housing substantially. Congressional appropriations for this type of renewal have been limited, but the major difficulty has come about because of ill-conceived, badly coordinated efforts between various levels of government. Certainly this type of renewal has been of little aid and/or value to the urban poor. Apart from displacing populations in vast numbers, developers and city planners have frequently replaced residential areas with nonresidential projects.[30] The Coliseum at Columbus Circle in New York City is one such example. Because the federal legislation does not require the construction of housing explicitly for the urban poor, what may have been the spirit of the program from a federal perspective became translated as it passed through various levels of government, ultimately allowing local authorities to do as they pleased as long as a slum area was in some manner rehabilitated.

Subsidized low-income public housing has similarly been problematic. Most projects financed through these funds have been constructed in inner cities. Local housing authorities direct these programs through the administration of the Public Housing Administration. From its inception in 1937 to date, this program has changed. Originally intended to aid in housing an urban middle-class population, it has come to be consigned to the urban poor. Again, the difficulty with implementation of this program is that on a national level there is recognition that housing for the poor must be provided. Funding for this program could not accurately be described as a national priority, but where such funds are available few local communities are receptive to such projects in their immediate neighborhoods. Relatively little of this type of housing has been constructed. Moreover, it has resulted in some of the most dramatic program failures on record. An outstanding example of excessive spending coupled with unmitigated failure was the Pruitt-Igoe project in St. Louis. Typically the project was populated by a high concentration of the urban poor. Constructed at a cost of thirty-six million dollars, the life span of the project was less than ten years. It was built in the late 1960s and closed down in 1973. Pruitt-Igoe is one of the more dramatic examples of the failure of subsidized housing programs. But the general results are much the same. What is well intended on a federal level frequently results in the creation of new ghettos when implementation on the local level takes place.

Evaluating mortgage insurance programs is difficult—historically they have been hailed as successful. These insurance programs were aimed at middle-income families with the intention of affording them the opportunity to become homeowners. This goal has been accomplished. However, since most of these potential home buyers have elected to live in suburban areas, these programs have certainly contributed to the maintenance of residential segregation.

Urban Homesteading is the least costly venture thus far proposed to reha-bilitate inner cities. As mentioned, most inner cities of the United States have an abundance of available abandoned housing. The cost of restoring this hous-ing to the local and federal governments is nonexistent. Whether or not the program is viable is another consideration. First, most of the housing has been abandoned because the neighborhoods in which it is located are particularly undesirable. As a result there is some question as to how many people will be willing to live and restore in these areas, even if the cost of the basic structure is nominal. Second, this housing cannot be transferred to willing individuals unless the particular city government holds title to the property. Many of the original owners are not present and accounted for, but they retain title to the property. Without being able to obtain clear title it is unlikely that many indi-viduals will risk spending the money required to rehabilitate such property.

Model Cities legislation was passed in 1966 and is broad-based, incorporat-ing the attempt to remedy a variety of urban ills along with housing problems. The directives for constructing a Model Cities plan is vague on a general level and means even less on a specific level. According to the legislation, "local communities" submit plans through three bureaucratic levels before they are approved for funding. The first difficulty arises when "local community" is defined. That is, it is never clear as to what constitutes the local community and how this representation is to be achieved. If a plan is presented it is then approved by a Model Cities central office, by the city's Board of Estimate, and ultimately by HUD in Washington. This program has been problematic because funding has not been adequate. Moreover, there have been local struggles con-cerning funding, control, personnel, and priorities.

It is difficult to argue that any of the federal housing programs, with the exception of mortgage insurance programs, have been successful. It is further difficult to argue that there have been any serious efforts made to provide adequate funding for these programs. However, few of these programs are designed for the urban poor in any case. The major difficulty, however, is that while the money for various programs is allocated by HUD, this agency neither plans nor implements the programs on a local level. As a result, what is presumably federal policy often becomes obscured as other levels of government enter the arena. If there is no implementation power on a federal level, it is not difficult to understand why private interests direct the housing market in the United States. Since the ultimate interest of private forces is the guarantee of profit, or at least the minimization of loss, it is not surprising that housing priorities are geared toward the interests of the middle- and upper-income groups and that the comfort of these groups is the ultimate goal. Thus, even if federal intent is to provide for poor populations, this intent must get lost between the planning and implementation stages of urban projects.

Race and Social Class

In the District the conflict concerning private urban renewal and displacement has emerged in racial terms. Endless conspiracy theories circulate with regularity. These theories suggest that there is a long-range plan in operation geared to drive blacks out of the city by 1990. When private urban renewal is discussed locally it is always in a racial context. The most frequent charge is that "reverse blockbusting" is being intentionally carried out by those determined to return the city to white control. Certainly there is evidence of black displacement accompanied by increased white owner occupancy in private urban renewal areas. The question is whether this represents a new form of conscious racial exclusion or if it is a function of economics. Moreover, the answer may not be easily found, because the issue of social class and race is problematic.

In every U.S. city there is a high correlation between race and poverty. This is not to argue that all the poor in central cities are black, nor that all blacks are poor. However, poverty among black populations is disproportionately high when compared to the numbers that comprise the black population. Additionally it is difficult to measure social class due to the difficulty of selecting appropriate and/or consistent variables that can be applied to different populations. For example, social class is usually measured by devising some type of socioeconomic status index. Frequently these indexes are created by combining variables such as income, education, and occupational rank. If indexes can be devised, there still remains the question of whether blacks and whites can be categorized by using the same criteria. The trouble is, we know that blacks have been discriminated against in the areas of housing, job opportunity, educational access, and income. The median income hierarchy in the United States is such that for persons twenty-five years of age and over, white males lead with $9378 annually; black males follow with $5648; white women are next, earning $3073; and black women are last with $2730 per year.[31]

Obviously these inequities throw off the possibility of accurate classification of social class status, since we know that these differing salaries frequently are earned for the same occupational roles.[32] The result is that what may be described as middle class for a white population may not be automatically applied to blacks with any confidence in the accuracy of such a classification.

Social class is an issue that must be considered along with racial discrimination in residential housing patterns. Because of the historical existence of discrimination, residential segregation cannot be seen as a function of the economic market exclusively. For example, a black couple was awarded $12,500 recently in a law suit against a white realtor who refused to allow the couple to look at a house in an expensive white residential area of the District.[33] This is a single case, but it substantiates the general argument that even if blacks can afford to live in expensive areas they are frequently denied access because of racial considerations. As shown by the data analysis of the private urban renewal areas, the incoming white population is moving into census tracts that have been up to this time either areas that housed large black populations such as Georgetown, or areas that housed almost exclusively black populations such as Capitol Hill and Adams-Morgan. As the process continues these areas become increasingly white in population composition. There is no way to demonstrate whether this is an economic process or a function of race *per se*. Available data do not allow for a definitive assertion regarding this question. There is evidence to suggest that both economics and race are factors. This is probably a result of the population composition of this particular city. There is evidence from other cities across the country that indicates that poor whites and other ethnic groups also are being displaced.[34] The existing evidence for an economic argument is strong. First, given the median incomes of blacks and whites, if a white affluent population is electing to move into the inner city, there is probably little that can be done to prevent black expulsion from the areas. The reasons for this are mainly economic. The private urban renewal brings in a population that is capable, in large numbers, of raising the tax revenue base of the city. If the displaced population is forced out of the city, the welfare costs, unemployment costs, and social service costs are likely to be reduced. Additionally, if one examines the cost of housing and the required income to become a home-owner, it is clear that whites have the economic advantage.

There are similarities between the traditional blockbusting phenomenon and the private urban renewal process. Both blockbusting and private urban renewal are profit-producing enterprises. Realtors obviously spend considerable time listing property for sale with the intention of selling it to contractors or builders who will remodel it for resale at higher prices or who will move into the area themselves.

In traditional blockbusting situations blockbusters make an effort to open peripheral areas to black populations. In the case of private urban renewal, speculators purchase on the fringes with the intention of encouraging others to move into those areas and expand the process. Rather than suggesting that an area is deteriorating and becoming a poor investment, in the case of private urban renewal realtors must promote an area and indicate that it is a sound financial investment. Moreover, the presence of an incoming white population is hardly likely to set off a wave of panic, because it is unlikely that there is a tipping point in terms of white visibility. The presence of whites of middle-class status is more likely to elevate the quality of an area than it is to set off a wave of panic selling. Moreover, there is ample evidence to suggest that blacks in these areas are renters and not owners. As such, they have no power—they cannot stay if the buildings are sold for restoration. It is easy to understand how the black tenant population is moved out of an area. The removal of the black homeowning population is somewhat more complex. However, there is some evidence that this population as well moves as the process continues. What happens in the case of black homeowners is that as property in the immediate area is improved, tax assessments on their property rise as well. It is likely that ultimately these prices rise to the point where black homeowners can no longer afford to maintain the property.

Another dimension is the introduction of "concentrated code violation areas." When this type of practice is put into effect, areas are selected out and the city demands that all the violations on the property be removed. The cost of this type of repair is frequently beyond the economic power of the homeowning black. As costs rise it becomes difficult for the black homeowning population to resist selling and moving elsewhere.

Historically residential housing patterns in the United States have been homogeneous. Any number of factors combine to guarantee this condition. Among these factors are exclusionary zoning regulations; realtors directing people to areas deemed "appropriate" for their racial or economic statuses; and the attitudinal stance taken by the general population. It is unlikely that private urban renewal areas will be any different. At the outset there may be racial and economic integration. However, as the process proceeds it is doubtful that heterogeneity will be maintained. Historical and economic forces combine to mitigate against this possibility. The changes in the District are manfesting in racial terms, more likely by default than by design. Social class and economic considerations appear to be far more important than race. If these areas result in homogeneous inner city neighborhoods it will be in keeping with the economic system, which is pricing blacks and other poor populations out of these areas.

Notes

1. See, for example: *Miami Herald*, "Special Report on Housing," 5 August 1973; Rochelle L. Stanfield, "Cities Being Rehabilitated through

Housing Ills Remain," *National Journal,* July 17, 1976; George and Eunice Grier, "Movers to the City," Washington, D.C.: Washington Center for Metropolitan Studies, May 1977.

2. Eunice Grier and George Grier, *Black Suburbanization at the Mid-1970's* (Washington, D.C.: Washington Center for Metropolitan Studies, 1978).

3. This question was raised by Senator William Proxmire in *Hearings before the Committee on Banking, Housing and Urban Affairs,* Senate, July 7-8, 1977.

4. See, for example: Herbert J. Gans, *The Urban Villagers* (New York: Free Press, 1962); Daniel Thursz, "Where Are they Now?," Health and Welfare Council of the National Capital Area, 1969.

5. Marshall B. Clinard, *Slums and Community Development* (New York: Free Press, 1970), part I; Staughton Lynd, "Urban Renewal—For Whom?" *Commentary* 31 (January 1961): 33-45.

6. Paul F. Wendt, *Housing Policy—The Search for Solutions* (Berkeley, Calif.: University of California Press, 1962).

7. *Portfolio,* a quarterly newsletter, published by Walker and Dunlop, Washington, D.C., Winter 1978, p. 2.

8. Thomas J. Black, "Private Housing Renovation in Central Cities: A ULI Survey," *Urban Land,* vol. 34, no. 10 (November 1975).

9. *Wall Street Journal,* 4 January 1976.

10. *New York Times,* 11 June 1976.

11. *The Brownstoner,* vol. 9, no. 3 (June 1978).

12. Interview with Samuel J. Lefrak, *Washington Post,* 28 June 1975; This is confirmed by data available in *Current Housing Reports* Series H-150, Part A, *General Housing Characteristics, 1973-1975.*

13. *Displacement: City Neighborhoods in Transition* (Washington, D.C.: National Urban Coalition, 1978).

14. District of Columbia, Municipal Planning Office, June 1977.

15. *New York Times,* 20 June 1976.

16. *Washington Post,* 14 June 1973.

17. *Lusk's District of Columbia Real Estate Directory Service,* Washington, D.C., May 1972-June 1976, p. 111.

18. *Lusk's Real Estate Directory, Weekly Reports,* Washington, D.C., 1978.

19. *Report to the District Committee on Finance and Revenue,* April 1975.

20. *Public Hearings on the Real Estate Transaction Tax of 1975,* June 19, 1975.

21. *Public Hearings on the Real Estate Transaction Tax of 1975,* November 25, 1975.

22. Washington Residential Development Coalition *Newsletter,* vol. 1, undated.

23. Donald H. Bouma, "The Analysis of the Social Power Position of a Real Estate Board," *Social Problems* 10 Fall 1962, p. 118.

24. WRDC *Newsletter,* undated, p. 4.

25. Murray S. Stedman, Jr., *Urban Politics* (Cambridge, Mass.: Winthrop Publishers, 1975), p. 264.

26. Leonard Downie, Jr., *Mortgage on America* (New York: Praeger Publishers, 1974), p. 8.

27. *Cities: Where People Live and Why,* Episodes in Social Inquiry Series (Belmont, Calif.: Allyn and Bacon, 1973), p. 32.

28. Office of Statistical Standards, Executive Office of the President, Bureau of the Budget, *Standard Metropolitan Statistical Area's* (Washington, D.C.: Government Printing Office, 1967), p. 1.

29. U.S. Bureau of the Census of Governments, 1967, vol. 1, *Governmental Organization* (Washington, D.C.: Government Printing Office, 1968), p. 11.

30. Lawrence M. Friedman, *Government and Slum Housing* (Chicago: Rand McNally, 1968), p. 150.

31. *Women and Poverty,* Staff Report, United States Commission on Civil Rights, June 1976, p. 6.

32. Charmeynne D. Nelson, "Myths about Black Women Workers in Modern America," *The Black Scholar* (March 1975), p. 13.

33. *Washington Post,* 9 September 1977.

34. *Displacement,* National Urban Coalition.

7 Summary, Conclusions, and Discussion

Urban Change Indicators

There is no general theoretical framework within which to analyze the urban milieu. We do not know how and why neighborhoods change. We have not yet developed a battery of indicators that allow for predicting either neighborhood improvement or decline. A major handicap for the development of such a predictive device is that the most commonly used unit of analysis is the census tract. The census tract is the smallest areal unit for which comprehensive data are collected. However, census tracts are frequently too large to allow intensive examination of population composition. Moreover, they are artificially created districts that do not permit examination of within-tract population changes. It is possible that the majority of changes in a census tract take place in only a small part of the tract but are reflected as tractwide changes. Census data by tract are collected at ten-year intervals, which are too long and too gross to allow for close examination of population change. It is possible that change occurs at one single point in time and is not spread over ten-year periods. It is equally possible that change begins in one part of a census tract and then spreads throughout the entire tract. There may be natural barriers such as freeways, bridges, parks, and the like that prevent change occurring in one section from continuing to another.

Another handicap is the lack of consistent data across cities. Ideally an indicator for predicting change would be a composite index utilizing sales volume, price change, percentage of vacant housing, number of absentee owners, race and social class of homeowners, and number of building permits requested. All this information is useful when attempting to anticipate change in residential areas. However, cities do not collect these data in any consistent manner. In fact, there is no guarantee that all these data are collected in all cities. As a result there has been heavy reliance on "intuition" or popular media sources indicating that areas are in transition. By the time change is visible and reported in the newspapers, change is frequently near completion, and changes in the composition of the population are being reported. This latter information is of little value to planners and policy-makers who presumably need to be able to anticipate change before the population shifts. Anticipation of change is important, it would allow planners to intervene before problems become insurmountable. It would aid policy-makers. commercial lending institutions, and government officials in making educated estimates for the future. For example, it is wasteful to build public school facilities if there is not going to be a school-aged population in the area in the extended future. It is useless to provide services for the elderly in areas where there are no long-term elderly resident populations. What is being suggested is that by the time change in the population composition of a neighborhood can be measured, it is too late to plan for the area. What is needed is an indicator of change that predates population change. Populations do not move overnight. They do not spontaneously enter or leave areas. There are some changes that precede population shifts. Rather than focusing initially on demographic characteristics of the population when attempting to anticipate change, it is possible to isolate other variables that would indicate, on a continuing basis, changes in urban neighborhoods.

An examination utilizing two variables, sales activity and property price, shows that a finite number of possible patterns can emerge. Sales activity is measured by the actual number of residential transactions occurring in a given area over fixed periods of time; sales price is actual price paid. As shown in figure 7-1, utilizing these two variables we can discern four possible patterns. These two variables must be used with a degree of caution and measured against a norm. For example, sales price is closely connected to general economic trends. Thus, in inflationary periods it is anticipated that prices will rise. They should rise in accordance with inflation and can be adjusted to take inflation into account. They should rise in proportion to the "normal" sales prices in a given area. Sales activity must be measured by local activity patterns. National mobility patterns indicate that half of all American households move every five years. Obviously, cities vary in terms of mobility patterns. The District of Columbia, for example, is both the seat of the federal government and a university city. As such, it has a high rate of population mobility. Other cities may have far less population turnover than the District. What is presented as a measure of sales activity is the "normal" rate of turnover of residential housing

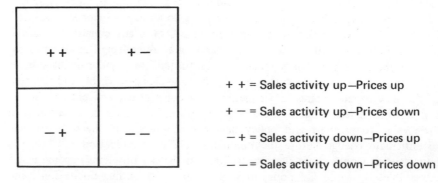

Figure 7-1. Urban Residential Change Indicators

in a particular urban area, with the recognition that local conditions will vary.

Utilizing these two variables has unique advantages: First, most cities have these data readily available. Second, this approach can be used on a census tract level, but it is not limited to that level of analysis. It can easily be reduced to a block level of analysis as well. These two variables can, by no means, explain what is changing or why change is taking place beyond the dimensions of their own definitions. However, they can be utilized to signal where change is taking place, and they can be applied at continuous intervals. For example, if sales activity is down or stable and prices are high and static, no change is going on in the area. This is based on the assumption that sales activity in the area approximates the citywide activity pattern, and that prices are adjusted for inflation. The same holds for the three other patterns; that is, activity down and price down may be the signal that an area is in the process of deterioration. Activity up and price static or down may be indicative of an area about to improve. Increased sales activity without price change may show that speculative buying is occurring in anticipation of area change. When activity is up and sales price is up as well, the area may be rapidly improving. If we superimpose these patterns on the private urban renewal process in the District, Georgetown is revealed as stable; that is, activity is low and prices are high. The tracts located close to the Capitol building on Capitol Hill indicate the same pattern. The tracts further out on Capitol Hill are experiencing both high activity and high prices. In Adams-Morgan there is a great deal of sales activity, but the prices are only beginning to rise.

Utilizing these two variables does not provide a great deal of information without further examination of a variety of other factors in a specific locale. However, this analysis can be used to identify areas of a city where differing patterns are emerging. Additionally, it can be used to keep a running account of what is happening in any given area regarding sales activity and price. Once the signal that something is changing occurs, it is possible to examine the area in depth.

Urban Decay: A Brief Synopsis

To discuss current changes it is necessary to review historical patterns. That is, before considering why inner city living is emerging as a desirable living pattern for some segments of the population, a brief review of the circumstances leading to urban decline is appropriate. Between 1955 and 1975, urban blight is the mode. This is the period during which most existing urban deterioration occurred. Without recapitulating the entire process and results of inner city deterioration, it is possible to provide a brief sketch of the history of this period. In order to account for inner city abandonment by those who were affluent

enough to leave, we must consider suburban development. The history of
suburban development predates 1955. The single most important factor in the
commencement of this trend was the advent of the automobile. This invention
allowed those of higher income to move from the inner city to the fringe areas.
The initial population movement was from the core of the city to the periphery.
During the 1920s, the impact of the automobile on population mobility was
clear. At this time upper income suburbs were beginning to emerge, and by the
mid-1920s, subdivisions were being laid out in the suburbs, preparing the ground-
work for future expansion. Black mobility following World War II contributed
to further suburban migration on the part of the white population. Recall that
in 1940, more than 50 percent of the black population lived in rural areas;
by 1970 three out of five blacks lived in central cities.[1] Certainly the 1954
Supreme Court school desegregation decision accelerated white flight out of
the cities.[2]

It is probably fair to say that most Americans appear to be content with
maintaining widespread disparities among racial and social classes in residential
housing patterns. It is certainly clear that the "melting pot" has not yet managed
to incorporate blacks and other poor minority groups. Suburban development
has provided a means by which racial and social class discrimination can be
maintained with a minimum of fuss. There are other reasons for suburban
development apart from exclusionary motives. First, as population declines in
inner cities, the supply of housing becomes far greater than the demand. This
creates price uncertainty and instability. Lending institutions become cautious,
and they are reluctant to invest in the inner city. Absentee ownership increases
as people move to the suburbs, renting the property they left behind. There is
increased tax delinquency, property abandonment occurs, the financial base of
city governments is weakened, and ability to provide public services is reduced.
Furthermore, Americans do not appear to be committed to city living in the
same manner as Europeans.[3] Rather, they embrace the notion of private property and have accepted the vision of their own detached house and plot of land
as the most desirable way of life. Whether this latter factor is a result or a
cause of suburban expansion is difficult to sort out at this time. However, the
fact is that the United States is a nation of suburbanites.

Despite population losses, urban expenditures have risen over time. There
are few urban governments without fiscal problems. Public expenditures have
always been significantly higher in urban than in nonurban areas, and this
trend has not been slowed by loss of population. In fact, as a result of loss
of middle-income population urban areas have been forced to assume an un-
equal share of the costs of services to the poor. The main source of revenue for
both local and city governments are property taxes. However, the revenue
accumulated from such taxes is not enough to cover the fiscal costs of maintaining city services. Moreover, these taxes do not increase enough to keep
abreast of fiscal demands. Because of the nature of the property tax structure

cities are at a disadvantage in terms of revenue raising. This tax structure is such that individuals are penalized for keeping their homes in good repair and rewarded for allowing housing conditions to deteriorate. The reason for this is that the property tax is actually two taxes combined. One dimension of the tax is the land value per se. That is, this is based on what the property would be worth if nothing had ever been done to improve it. The second dimension of the tax is on improvements. Therefore, unimproved property is taxed at lower rates than is improved property. This, of course, aids in encouraging slum landlords and inhibits private investment in property upkeep. In addition, it deters restoration and/or the building of housing for low- and moderate-income groups because of the additional tax costs on repairs and/or new construction. For example, a property may be slated for construction in one year at a given cost. Before it is completed the cost of materials and labor may have doubled. Since property cannot be appraised from the drawing board it must be appraised upon completion. During the time taken for construction costs as well as taxes may have doubled. Because property taxes are not related to ability to pay, individuals who are not priced out of the market may well be taxed out of the same market. This is further complicated by the fact that urban taxes are generally higher than nonurban taxes at the outset. Nonetheless these taxes do not provide enough revenue to meet the needs of the cities. Raising the taxes is no solution, because it contributes to driving those who are able to pay out of the city, thus reducing the tax base further. Cities have been receiving more aid from state and federal governments in the recent past, but their inability to resolve property tax structure from within has certainly contributed to urban decay.

Private Urban Renewal: A Different Trend

Georgetown is a prototype, illustrating how the process of private urban renewal in the District has resulted in the following changes to the renewal area:

1. Loss of total population in the areas experiencing the renewal process.
2. Increased median family income.
3. Median level of education has risen.
4. Both black renter and black homeowner population have decreased.
5. Increased white owner occupancy.
6. Dramatically increased peoperty values, unmatched in the balance of the city.

The components of the private urban renewal process are:

1. Pioneers call attention to a particular area.

2. Real estate agents become involved and committed to inner city sales; speculators and builders follow.
3. Lending institutions enter the area.
4. Area property owners achieve local control over zoning decisions and/or Historical Preservation status.

This pattern is substantiated by reports on private urban renewal from across the country.[4] In the District this process is no longer confined to the areas under examination but has spread to other areas such as Mount Pleasant, Dupont Circle East, and Shaw. It is possible that the process is more completely developed in the District than it is in other cities. But, it is equally possible that this only appears to be the case because it has created serious conflicts in this city. There is little question, however, that this is a phenomenon occurring in most of the major cities of the country. Reasons for the emergence of this process are discussed next.

National Considerations

Having argued that urban areas do not exist in a vacuum and that analysis of urban areas devoid of political, economic, and social conditions is sterile, it is necessary to address the national level factors that contribute to the process of private urban renewal. In other words, what are the most broad considerations contributing to the desirability of inner city living for a certain segment of the population? A series of factors contributing to this process can be isolated and identified.

One of the first considerations is housing supply. The peak period of new housing construction in the United States was reached in 1970. Since that time, the rate of new housing construction has fallen to close to two million units per year. This represents a dramatic drop since 1970, and the result is that the demand for housing is running well ahead of capacity to supply.[5] Taken in isolation, this factor does not appear adequate to motivate a return to inner city living. However, cost is a related consideration. Cost is two-dimensional. Part of the reason that new construction has fallen off dramatically is that it is too expensive. From the builders' perspective, inflation is such that new housing construction costs are prohibitive. In a ten-year period, costs have accelerated such that the sales price required for the builder to profit has doubled. In addition, cost to the consumer is prohibitive. The median value of suburban owner-occupied dwellings increased by 50 percent during a single decade.[6] The general rule of thumb in residential purchases is that a buyer can afford a house priced at 2.5 times his annual income. This rule neglects consideration of interest rates, down payment, and monthly payments. Taking all these factors into account, if a family income is $50,000 per year, the buyer should be able to afford a home costing \$115,000 to \$127,000 at 8.5 percent interest with monthly payments of \$1040 and a down payment of approximately \$24,500. As interest rates rise, the housing cost must decline if all other factors remain equal.[7] Given this type of cost despite the above-average family income, it is clear that the combination of lack of new construction and high housing prices are national considerations that must be seriously weighed when attempting to explain private urban renewal. In fact, many analysts of housing trends have suggested that inflation might prohibit home buying, particularly among younger populations.[8]

Other national considerations include the fact that the "baby boom" generation born between 1940 and 1960 is now coming of home-buying age. This large potential home-purchasing population adds pressure to a housing market unable to meet even existing demands. Other considerations of a national scale include the fact that two-career families are increasingly the norm.[9] Women are delaying the birth of their first child or electing to not have children at all.[10] There has been and continues to be a threat of energy shortages, and the costs of heating fuel and gasoline increasingly rise. In addition, some of the original motivation for moving to the suburbs may no longer be applicable. There is increased evidence that the quality of public education is declining in both inner city and suburban areas. We are now in the process of busing school children on a national scale to achieve school integration. Moreover, there appears to be a growing disenchantment with suburban living as more and more of what were formerly perceived to be urban social problems emerge in suburban areas.

It is not difficult to isolate the national changes that have occurred in the past two decades. It is very evident that there have been major changes in the social and economic fabric of the society. However, interpreting the effect of these changes in relation to the process of private urban renewal is both difficult and speculative. These interpretations must be considered empirical questions, because there has been little examination of the attitudes of the population that are becoming homeowners in the inner city. To examine national level considerations in relation to this population, it is important to recall that all available data indicate that this group is composed of white, young, professional, single people or couples without children. Given this portrait of the population, a number of possible explanations for why they are becoming homeowners in the inner city can be offered. As a young population, this group is probably in the initial stages of career development and not yet earning sizeable incomes. As a result, the inner city may appear far more appealing than suburban housing, because prior to 1973, housing costs in the inner city not only lagged far behind suburban costs but inflated at a much slower pace.[11] In addition, there was more available housing stock in the inner cities during this period. If two people are working, it is far more convenient to live in the city than to commute. The saving can be measured in terms of both time and cost. There is a saving in fuel expense, since attached row houses are less expensive and less difficult to heat than are detached houses. If people are delaying the birth of their first child or electing not to have children, the quality of public schools is not a concern. Additionally, there is no longer any guarantee that one's children will go to a neighborhood school, thus reducing the importance of school district as a factor in housing choice. There is increased crime in suburban areas. They are no longer free of drug problems, juvenile delinquency, or vandalism. There is some evidence that these problems are mounting rapidly and that the suburbs are no longer a haven from the problems of the city. A further consideration is attitude. The "baby boom" generation may find suburban living completely unappealing. There is reason to believe that this generation may not share the values of their parents—having grown up in the suburbs themselves, they may elect different life-styles as adults. That there have been many changes on a national level cannot be debated. How these changes are affecting the population involved in the process of private urban renewal remains an empirical question, which should receive continued attention.

Regional Considerations

Changes occurring on a national level affect the total population. Urban areas, however, are not identical across the country. The dynamics that contribute to the process of private urban renewal probably vary from one locale to another. The considerations that are taken into account in relation to this process in the District must be confined to the Washington, District of Columbia, Standard Metropolitan Statistical Area (SMSA). Accounting for the process in other cities requires an analysis grounded in knowledge about the area under examination.

In the Washington SMSA a number of factors help to explain the emergence of the process of private urban renewal. These factors have to do with regional and city actions that affect the population of the area. For example, the District has instituted a policy of requiring residential parking permits. This has created a serious problem for commuters, who were accustomed to driving into the District to work and parking free on the street. Now, they can park their cars for a maximum of two hours. The District traffic control department has implemented this policy with rigor; commuters are now forced to pay for parking facilities. It is likely that many young people who were formerly willing to commmute have now considered moving into the city rather than paying the expense of parking.

Another factor, and probably one that is considerably more serious, is that until recently there have been sewer moratoria in the two outlying counties closest to the District line. Because of overdevelopment, these areas no longer have the capacity to expand treatment facilities for the disposal of waste material. Thus, building has been halted because it is not possible to hook up sewer lines. The result is that it is necessary to go further out in suburbia to buy a new house. This, of course, increases both time and cost of commuting.

Suburban housing costs have risen higher than those of the District. Median value is not the best measure, because it is based on the current owner's assessment of what the house would sell for if it was put on the market. However, it provides a measure of differences in cost in this region. The estimated median value of residential houses in Montgomery County and Prince George's County, respectively, are $55,100 and $39,200. These figures are considerably higher than the median value of $30,600 recorded in the District.[12]

State and local tax structures are another consideration. The District, of course, has no state tax. As a result, state and local taxes for a family of four with an income of $15,000 in 1975 are also higher in the surrounding counties than in the District. In Montgomery County taxes estimated on this basis amount to $626. The same is true of Prince George's County. The comparable figure in the District is $493.[13]

The counties that are closest to the District have begun to bus for school integration this year. In the past, the Montgomery County public school system was considered one of the best in the country, but there is much local trepidation concerning its fate now that busing has been instituted. In this same county there have been a series of drug arrests in the public high schools in the recent past. Thus, the urban ills appear less escapable.

Perhaps a major incentive to inner city home buying in this particular locale is that until recently there was a 7.5 percent ceiling on mortgage lending interest rates. In the surrounding areas the ceiling is 10 percent. As a result, the interest rate on home purchases was lower in the District than in the surrounding suburbs.

The City of Washington, District of Columbia

It may well be that one of the major considerations in relation to the private urban renewal process in the District is its visible success. In this city it is possible to point to Georgetown and Capitol Hill as illustrations of what can be accomplished. This probably provides a great deal of incentive to those interested in accelerating the process and aiding in its spread to other areas of the city. Perhaps the most succinct way to discuss the process of private urban renewal is by asking the question, "How can this process be stimulated in an urban area where it has not yet occurred? That is, what combination of factors must be present for private urban renewal to occur?" Superficially this appears to be a three-stage process. The stages are: pioneers move into an area; they are followed by realtors who promote the area until it is well developed; then an affluent population arrives and the process is underway. However, the dynamics are more complex. A combination of factors must be present for private urban renewal to take place. Figure 7-2 depicts the factors involved in the process. First, a city must contain a substantial, old, well-constructed housing stock. It is preferable that some of this housing stock be of historical interest, but this is not essential. Without solid housing stock there is nothing to restore. Additionally, the city must have the capacity to employ a sizeable group of professional and/or managerial people. This capacity is necessary because housing costs rise sharply once the process has commenced. At first glance, this appears tautological. That is, professionals are moving into the inner cities; therefore the cities must be able to support a professional population. However, this is not so circular as it originally appears. Professional populations are well educated, and education mitigates against prejudices and stereotypical thinking.[14] Thus, on the dimension of attitude, if any population is likely to consider urban living by choice it is this group. The third dimension is absentee ownership, which is automatically accompanied by high vacancy rates or tenant populations. If housing costs are a consideration for those buying in the inner city, there has to be an available supply. It is difficult to imagine the private urban renewal process occurring in a stable residential community. Moreover, one of the important conditions that contributes both to the maintenance of housing and social stability is home ownership.[15] Therefore, it would appear that private urban renewal has to take place in an area where the existing population can be displaced. Another factor is that the process must take place in a period of housing scarcity or in a locale where the housing market is "tight." If there is a scarcity of housing in surrounding areas, it is likely that inner city housing will appear desirable.

The first stage in the private urban renewal process is the arrival of "pioneers." These are people who usually have limited financial resources and do a considerable amount of the actual property rehabilitation themselves. In Bay Village, Boston, the pioneer group was a gay community; in Park Slope, Brooklyn, it was an artistic community; in Capitol Hill it was young couples who wanted to live in the city.[16] For an area to gain popularity and to be promoted widely as "up and coming," pioneers must be followed by realtors, speculators, and builders. The role of the realtor is to advertise and promote the positive qualities of the neighborhood and to encourage and increase the incoming population. The role of speculators and builders is to rapidly expand the area, thereby making housing available for those who are relatively more affluent and thus less inclined to "do it themselves" than the earliest settlers.

If the private urban renewal process is to continue, local lending institutions must be willing to invest in the inner city. This investment is usually forthcoming as soon as the particular area appears to be improving. Moreover, realtors are usually connected to lending institutions, which will make loans in the inner city when enough private capital has been invested in the area to minimize their risk. Thereafter, population must continue to grow, and the

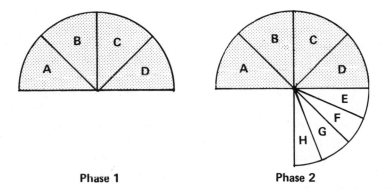

Phase 1   Phase 2

Phase 3

A. Solid housing stock

B. City with capacity to
employ professional and/or
managerial population

C. Absentee ownership with
vacant housing and/or tenant
population

D. "Tight" housing market

E. "Pioneers"

F. Realtors

G. Speculators

H. Contractors & builders

I. Lending institutions

J. "City conscious" population

K. Local control of zoning

L. Affluent population

Figure 7-2. Private Urban Renewal Model

home-buying population must increase. This home-buying population is obviously somewhat special, and it has been described as "city conscious" for want of better terminology. What this actually means is that this population must be willing to make both personal and financial commitments to inner city living. The reason for stressing this factor is that private urban renewal areas are neither initially attractive nor inherently desirable. The pioneers obviously experience the worse circumstances, but until the process is well underway these areas are not generally pleasant. Frequently, new single-family owners live next door to multiple-family groups. The areas they are moving into are dirty, littered with glass and garbage. They are noisy and, often, actually dangerous. Thus the incoming population must be comprised of people who can live with these conditions temporarily, assuming that ultimately conditions will improve. The financial risk is, of course, minimized over time. For the pioneer group the risk is maximal, since the success of the process depends on their being followed by others. For the latecomers the financial risk is minimal, because housing costs tend to rise dramatically once the process is underway. Thus, if the process is successful, those who entered the area first may have risked the most, but they stand to gain more, because they purchased at a time when property prices were relatively low. Those who enter later tend to pay premium prices for housing, but property values seem to continue to rise.

Gaining local control over zoning is, of course, a prime factor in accelerating improvements, but this control does not exist in the initial stages of the private urban renewal process. It is clearly important to the long-term rehabilitation of the area, because it does allow the community to decide the course of its own future. Moreover, if Historical Preservation status can be attained, an area is virtually free of outside intervention. Zoning has been used in suburban communities as an exclusionary device. It is clear that it can potentially be used for the same purposes in private urban renewal areas. Historical Designation is also an important dimension to the process. It is reported that this status has been requested by a large number of private urban renewal areas in various cities across the country. Milton Kotler reports that the term *historical preservation* has come to be a fighting word in many areas.[17]

In the final stage of private urban renewal, prices rise, populations change, and living conditions improve dramatically. When this occurs entrance to the area becomes limited to the relatively affluent, and pioneers are forced to seek new places to begin the process again.

It is difficult to discuss what type of city is receptive to the process of private urban renewal beyond the factors mentioned. It is conceivable that city type is limiting. That is, cities such as Newark, New Jersey, may be too deteriorated for the renewal process to take place. There were once areas of Newark that contained solid housing stock, but much of the original building of that city was frame wood construction. As a result, it is unlikely that there is much left to rehabilitate. There are other cities that have experienced little deterioration, and the sections that have decayed are fairly limited. Providence, Rhode Island, is one such city. Within the central city are large, detached frame houses that have withstood the strains of time. The areas that have deteriorated are contained geographically. Since this is a city where housing prices have gradually inflated, it is still possible to purchase property at reasonable cost; as a result there is no reason to restore the deteriorated sections. In Philadelphia, Pennsylvania, the private urban renewal process is occurring in some sections. However, it is a slow, gradual process, because the city does not have a scarcity of residential housing. Clearly, different urban patterns are dominant in urban areas across the country. Whether or not the process of private urban renewal will occur depends very much on local and regional conditions.

That the private urban renewal process is occurring on a national level is a fact. It represents a population trend that had not been predicted and one that runs counter to the dominant population movement of the past two decades. The process is having an impact on the immediate areas in which it is occurring, although the dimensions of its significance on a citywide level remain to be seen. Exactly what is occurring is unclear. That is, we know that certain areas of the inner cities are being restored. We know that a white, relatively affluent population is replacing a poor population. We do not know whether or not this represents a "return-to-the-city" movement. We have some evidence that it represents a "stay-in-the-city" movement, but even this is speculative and based on limited investigation. The process presents many positive aspects. Certain sections of inner cities are being rehabilitated and converted into pleasant residential areas. But the process is not without negative features. It is displacing populations wherever it is occurring, and this displacement promises to add to existing social problems. Despite these shortcomings, private urban renewal is the first success among many efforts to rehabilitate inner cities. Private urban renewal is being successfully accomplished in areas where public expenditure efforts have failed. Neither urban renewal programs nor subsidized housing programs had significant impact in regard to reversing the cycle of urban decay. The department of HUD has recently announced that it is discontinuing the New Cities program. Urban homesteading is unlikely to make a major impact on inner cities, and Model Cities programs remain to be evaluated.

In a statement before the U.S. Senate Committee on Banking, Housing and Urban Affairs, Franklin James stated, "Unless curtailed by national policy, private economic forces appear certain to continue to produce high levels of housing demand and reinvestment in central city housing."[18] It is entirely possible that his assertion is correct. Additionally, reinvestment in central city housing may provide living quarters that are no longer available or affordable in suburban areas. If this proves to be the case, inner cities may return to viable fiscal condition. A number of forces have combined to make new construction of housing and replacement of housing losses difficult if not impossible. Costs of land close enough to city center have risen dramatically. Labor and building material costs as well as lack of mortgage funds, high interest rates, and inflation of housing costs have all contributed to the decline of new construction. As a result, the private urban renewal of the inner city may offer a partial solution to providing for the nation's housing needs. Thus far it appears that this process is providing for the needs of the middle class. In the District of Columbia the consequence is removal of the poor, primarily black population. This dimension of private urban renewal may be unique to cities where severe housing shortages exist. Displacement may not be an issue in cities where there is an ample housing supply available. Perhaps the greatest opportunity presented by the emergence of the private urban renewal process is the potential for achieving racial and social integration on a voluntary basis. That is, at a given point in time this racial and social integration exists because the new population has not totally displaced the existing population in any given neighborhood. As the process continues displacement occurs. Rather than curtail the process it would seem that this is an opportunity for local and federal governments to intervene and assist in the maintenance of the heterogeneity that has to exist for a certain period of time. Further examination of the process of private urban renewal in a variety of cities is required before policy decisions can adequately be made. However, if the process continues and accelerates, a variety of innovative housing programs could be devised and implemented that would contribute to creating both varied inner city neighborhoods as well as economically viable communities.

Notes

1. Anthony Downs, *Urban Problems and Prospects* (Chicago: Markham Publishing Company, 1970), p. 29.

2. *Brown et. al.* vs. *Board of Education of Topeka et. al,* Supreme Court verdict rendered May 17, 1954.

3. See, for example: Morton White and Lucia White, *The Intellectual Versus the City* (Cambridge, Mass: Harvard University Press, 1962), pp. 13-14; William Kane Reilly, "Conservation, Community, and Personal Responsibility," in *Social Science and Urban Crisis,* eds. Victor B. Ficker and Herbert S. Graves, (New York: Macmillan Publishing Co., Inc., 1978), pp. 307-320.

4. "Neighborhood Diversity," *Hearings before the Committee on Banking, Housing and Urban Affairs,* U.S. Senate, 95th Congress, July 7 and 8, 1977.

5. U.S. Department of Housing and Urban Redevelopment, *Housing in the Seventies: A Report of the National Housing Policy Review* (Washington, D.C.: Government Printing Office, 1974), table 2.

6. U.S. Bureau of the Census, Census of Housing, *Metropolitan Housing Characteristics: United States and Regions,* 1974.

7. "Househunter's Guide," Family Housing Bureau, Chicago Title Insurance Company, Illinois 1977.

8. See, for example, Raymond J. Struyk, *Urban Homeownership* (Lexington, Mass.: Lexington Books, D.C. Heath and Co., 1976), chapter 7.

9. U.S. Department of Commerce, *Statistical Abstract of the United States, 1972* (Washington, D.C.: Government Printing Office, 1972), table 348, p. 222.

10. See, for example, Juanita M. Kreps, *Women and the American Economy: A Look to the 1980's,* American Assembly, Columbia University, 1976.

11. U.S. Bureau of the Census, *Annual Housing Survey,* part C, "Financial Characteristics of the Housing Inventory, 1974" (Washington, D.C.: Government Printing Office, 1974).

12. Washington Region 1974, "Population and Housing Data from Washington Area Census Updating System" (Washington, D.C.: Washington Center for Metropolitan Studies, 1974), p. 57.

13. District of Columbia Data, "Major State and Local Tax Burdens for a Family of Four Residing in Selected Washington Metropolitan Are Jurisdictions, 1975" (Washington, D.C.: Municipal Planning Office, 1976), p. 21.

14. Leonard Broom and Philip Selznick, "Socialization", in *Sociology* (New York: Harper and Row, 1973), p. 371.

15. See George Sternlieb and Robert Burchell, *Residential Abandonment: The Tenant Landlord Revisited* (New Brunswick, N.J.: Rutgers University Center for Urban Policy Research, 1972).

16. Rolf Goetze, "Local Issues in Neighborhood Conservation and Housing Rehabilitation," U.S. Senate Hearings, 1977, p. 225.

17. Milton Kotler, Executive Director of National Association of Neighborhoods, U.S. Senate Hearings, 1977, p. 183.

18. Franklin James, "Neighborhood Diversity" Hearings before the Committee on Banking, Housing and Urban Affairs, U.S. Senate, 95th Cong., July 7 and 8, 1977.

**Appendix A
District of Columbia
Census Tracts**

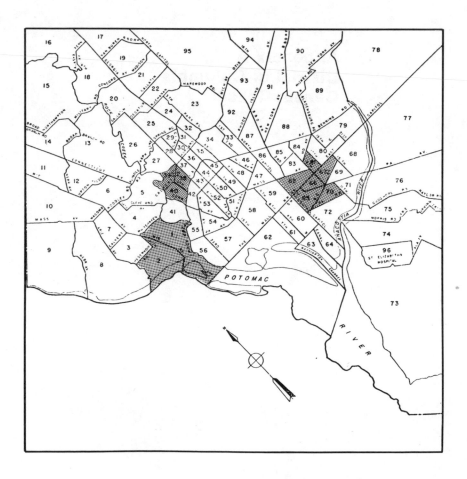

Designates Georgetown, Capitol Hill and Adams Morgan tracts

**Appendix B
Private Urban Renewal
Census Tracts**

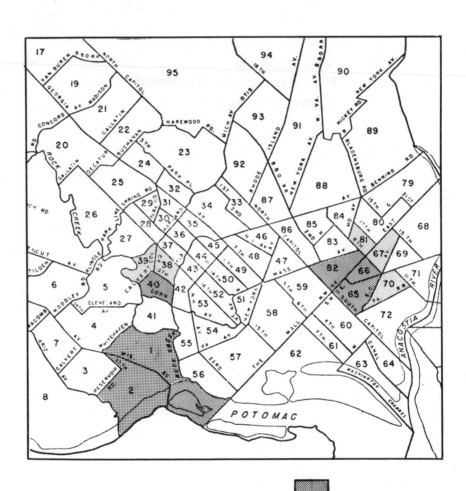

Restoration tracts

Transition tracts

Appendix C
Racial Composition of the Population of the District of Columbia, 1800–1970

Decade	Percent Black	Percent White	Total Population
1800	23	77	3,210
1810	28	72	8,208
1820	27	73	13,247
1830	29	71	18,827
1840	28	72	23,364
1850	26	74	40,001
1860	18	82	61,122
1870	32	68	109,199
1880	34	66	177,624
1890	33	67	230,392
1900	31	69	278,718
1910	29	71	331,069
1920	25	75	437,571
1930	27	73	486,869
1940	28	72	663,091
1950	35	65	802,178
1960	55	45	763,956
1970	72	28	756,510

Source: Compiled from U.S. Census Bureau, *General Characteristics of the Population, Decennial Censuses* (Washington, D.C.: U.S. Government Printing Office, 1800-1970).

Appendix D
Percentage Black
Population by Census
Tract, 1940–1970

Tract Numbers	Time Intervals			
	1940	1950	1960	1970
Georgetown				
1	28	17	5	3
2	14	8	1	1
Capitol Hill				
65	24	38	46	27
66	11	20	24	22
67	16	32	70	74
70	20	33	69	54
81	7	25	76	88
82	10	16	22	17
Adams-Morgan				
38	41	42	54	76
39	3	3	10	54
40	18	25	31	27

Note: Percentages have been devised from numerical counts.

**Appendix E
Median Income of
Families in Private Urban
Renewal Tracts and
Citywide, 1950–1970**

Year	Citywide	Georgetown		Capitol Hill						Adams-Morgan		
		1	2	65	66	67	70	81	82	38	39	40
1950[a]	3,800[b]	3,900	1,400[c]	2,600	2,800	3,000	3,000	2,700	2,700	2,900	3,500	3,000
1960	6,000	11,400	9,800	5,800	5,400	4,500	4,700	6,000	6,000	5,000	6,000	6,000
1970	9,600	21,600	21,300	14,200	14,000	7,000	5,500	13,000	13,000	5,600	7,900	9,600

[a]These data were not collected in 1940.
[b]Numbers have been rounded to nearest $100.
[c]Data indicate that one-third of the population in this tract has family income under $500.

**Appendix F
Median Years of School
Completed By Census
Tract and Citywide,
1940–1970**

Year	Citywide	Georgetown		Capitol Hill						Adams-Morgan		
		1	2	65	66	67	70	81	82	38	39	40
1940	10.2	11	8.7	8.6	9.7	9.0	7.9	9.0	10.3	11.1	12.8	12.6
1950	12.2	12.9	12.5	9.6	9.8	9.6	8.3	9.8	11.3	12.3	12.7	12.7
1960	11.7	14.9	15.6	11.3	12.6	8.9	8.4	8.9	12.0	11.3	11.6	12.1
1970	12.2	16.3	16.6	14.0	14.2	10.0	12.1	10.2	13.3	11.8	12.4	12.7

**Appendix G
Percentage White
Homeowners by Census
Tract and Citywide,
1940-1970**

Year	Citywide	Georgetown		Capitol Hill						Adams-Morgan		
		1	2	65	66	67	70	81	82	38	39	40
1940	85	87	96	81	93	90	91	94	96	35	100	94
1950	74	91	98	69	84	73	59	74	89	42	99	86
1960	52	94	99	63	87	39	42	32	85	37	91	78
1970	38	97	100	73	89	50	71	22	89	41	85	84

**Appendix H
Ownership by Race by
Census Tract and
Citywide, 1940–1970**

	Georgetown				Capitol Hill												Adams-Morgan						Citywide	
	1		2		65		66		67		70		81		82		38		39		40			
Year	B	W	B	W	B	W	B	W	B	W	B	W	B	W	B	W	B	W	B	W	B	W	B	W
1940	72	503	15	381	85	372	17	240	74	578	32	312	25	418	13	368	79	43	0	207	17	251	7,670	44,274
1950	70	669	12	553	200	294	43	234	185	513	176	258	121	372	46	358	104	76	3	345	45	272	18,928	53,434
1960	50	841	4	599	171	286	37	257	357	230	206	152	307	146	59	326	122	74	41	451	97	348	36,042	39,532
1970	26	825	2	648	127	345	35	280	320	324	102	252	279	81	35	279	74	52	59	350	63	341	44,758	28,547

B = black; W = white

Appendix I
Percentage White Renter-Occupied Units by Census Tract and Citywide, 1940–1970

Year	Georgetown		Capitol Hill						Adams-Morgan			Citywide
	1	2	65	66	67	70	81	82	38	39	40	
1940	74	85	75	90	85	79	95	92	71	97	85	74
1950	90	91	73	87	76	85	88	91	69	98	82	72
1960	97	97	68	82	41	36	39	87	59	94	74	57
1970	98	97	84	80	32	47	18	85	30	37	70	35

Appendix J
Sample Selection and Description
of Respondents

Real estate brokerages were selected from Sunday open-house advertisements in the *Washington Post*. These advertisements were traced from 1970 to 1976. Between 1970 and 1973 agencies operating in private urban renewal areas were almost entirely city-based offices. After 1973 numerous suburban real estate companies began to advertise open houses in the private urban renewal areas of the District. The sample of brokerages was limited to those based in the District.

An examinatiion of the perceptions of forty participants in the real estate business was conducted. Two people were interviewed from each agency selected; one broker or office manager and one salesperson. Realtors interviewed began their operations at different times between 1950 and 1976.

There are twenty-six real estate companies in Capitol Hill alone. In the period 1950 to 1958 four real estate companies opened in the Capitol Hill area. Two of these companies were not new to the city. They were new to Capitol Hill. Prior to opening offices in Capitol Hill both these companies had offices in Georgetown and Foggy Bottom. The other two companies were opening for the first time. Since 1950 a total of twenty-two other real estate brokerages have opened on Capitol Hill. Almost all these companies are outgrowths of the original four companies. That is, almost all the twenty-two brokerages were started by agents who had formerly worked with another Capitol Hill agency before beginning their own business. When questioned about the number of real estate companies in this area, all the respondents indicated that there was more than enough business to go around. All stated that they could imagine still more agencies opening in the area. They claimed that even if offices are based on Capitol Hill, they are involved in the process of private urban renewal all over the city. The other offices where interviews were conducted are located in Georgetown, Adams-Morgan, and Dupont Circle.

All the respondents were white. The majority of the sales staff in every office where interviews were conducted were white. The age of respondents ranges from twenty-seven to fifty-five-years old. The level of education of respondents ranges from high school graduate to some graduate school education. Size of companies ranged from four to twenty employees. The gross income of respondents ranged from ten thousand dollars for a woman who was in the business for one year to seventy-five thousand dollars for a broker who has been in the business for eleven years.

Bibliography

Abrams, Charles. *Forbidden Neighbors*. New York: Harper Brothers, 1955.
_____. *Home Ownership for the Poor*. New York: Praeger Publishers, 1970.
_____. "Invasion and Counterattack," in *Violence in America*. Edited by Thomas Rose. New York: Vintage Books, 1970, pp. 181-192.

Adler, Bill. *Washington: A Reader*. New York: Meredith Press, 1967.

Adrian, Charles R. *Public Attitudes and Metropolitan Decision Making*. Pittsburgh: University of Pittsburgh Press, 1962.

Anderson, Theodore R., and Egeland, Janice A. "Spatial Aspects of Social Area Analysis." *American Sociological Review* 26 (June 1961): 392-399.

Babcock, Richard F. *The Zoning Game*. Madison, Wisc.: University of Wisconsin Press, 1969.

Bagdikian, Ben. "The Five Different Washingtons," in *Washington: A Reader*. Edited by Bill Adler. New York: Meredith Press, 1967, pp. 257-262.

Baker, Ross K. "The Ghetto Writ Large: The Future of the American City." *Social Policy* 4 (January/February 1974): 22-29.

Bass, Ralph. "Prejudice Won't Make Us Sell Our Home." *Coronet* (July 1959), pp. 101-105.

Beale, Calvin L. *The Revival of Population Growth in Non-Metropolitan America*. Washington: Economic Research Division. U.S. Department of Agriculture, 1975.

Bell, Wendell. "Economic Family and Ethnic Status: An Empirical Test." *American Sociological Review* 20 (February 1955): 45-52.

Benson, Charles A. "A Test of Transition Theories." *The Residential Appraiser* (August 1958), pp. 6-11.

Bercovici, Konrad. *Around the World in New York*. New York: Century Company, 1924.

Bernard, Jessie. *The Sociology of Community*. Glenview, Ill.: Scott, Foresman and Company, 1973.

Berry, Brian J. L., and Rees, Philip H. "The Factorial Ecology of Calcutta." *American Journal of Sociology* 74 (March 1969): 445-491.

Bibliography on the Urban Crisis, A Publication of the National Clearinghouse for Mental Health Information. Washington, D.C.: National Institute of Mental Health, 1969.

Bibliography of the District of Columbia: Being a List of Maps, and Newspapers, Including Articles in Other Publications to 1898. Washington, D.C.: U.S. Government Printing Office, 1900.

Black, Thomas J. *Private-Market Housing Renovation in Central Cities: An Urban Land Institute Survey*. Washington, D.C.: Urban Land Institute, 1975.

Blumer, Herbert. "Social Science and the Desegregation Process," in *Racial Desegregation and Integration*. Edited by Ira De A. Reid. Philadelphia: The American Academy of Political and Social Science, 1956, pp. 137-143.

Bouma, Donald H. "The Analysis of the Social Power Position of a Real Estate Board." *Social Problems* 10 (Fall 1962): 116-128.

———. "The Legitimation of the Social Power Position of a Real Estate Board." *American Journal of Economics and Sociology* 21 (October 1962): 383-393.

Broom, Leonard, and Selznick, Philip. "Socialization," in *Sociology*. New York: Harper and Row, 1973.

Brown, Letitia Woods. *Free Negroes in the District of Columbia 1790-1846*. New York: Oxford University Press, 1972.

"Brownstone Hunter's Guide." New York: Consolidated Edison Publication, undated.

Brownstoner. 9 June 1978.

Bullough, Bonnie. "Alienation in the Ghetto." *American Journal of Sociology* 72 (March 1967): 469-478.

Burgess, Ernest W. "The Growth of a City: An Introduction to a Research Project," in *The City*. Edited by Robert E. Park, Ernest W. Burgess, and Roderick D. McKenzie. 4th edition. Chicago: University of Chicago Press, 1967, pp. 47-62.

———. *The Urban Community*. Chicago: University of Chicago Press, 1925.

Caemmerer, A. Paul. *A Manual on the Origin and Development of Washington*. Washington, D.C.: U.S. Government Printing Office, 1939.

Chinitz, Benjamin. "Contrasts and Agglomeration: New York and Pittsburgh," in *Urban Economics*. Edited by Ronald E. Grieson. Boston: Little, Brown and Company, 1973, pp. 26-27.

Cicourel, Aaron V. *Method and Measurement in Sociology*. New York: Free Press, 1964.

Clinard, Marshall B. *Slums and Community Development*. New York: Free Press, 1970.

Cochrane, Colin. "The Georgetown Story." *National Capitol Area Realty* (March 1959), pp. 11-18.

Dahl, Robert A. *Who Governs?* New Haven, Conn.: Yale University Press, 1961.

Davis, Goerge A., and Donaldson, O. Fred. *Blacks in the United States: A Geographic Perspective*. Boston: Houghton-Mifflin, 1975.

Deskin, Donald R. *Residential Mobility of Negroes in Detroit 1837-1965*. Detroit: Department of Geography, University of Michigan, 1962.

Displacement: City Neighborhoods in Transition. Washington, D.C.: National Urban Coalition, 1978.

District of Columbia. Alley Dwelling Authority. *Report of the Alley Dwelling Authority. Fiscal Years 1935-39*. Washington, D.C.: U.S. Government Printing Office, 1936-1940.

District of Columbia Data. "Major State and Local Tax Burdens for a Family of Four Residing in Selected Washington Metropolitan Area Jurisdictions." Washington, D.C.: Municipal Planning Office, 1976.

Downie, Leonard, Jr. *Mortgage on America.* New York: Praeger Publishers, 1974.

Downs, Anthony. *Urban Problems and Prospects.* Chicago: Markham Publishing Company, 1971.

Drake, St. Clair, and Cayton, Horace R. *Black Metropolis: A Study of Negro Life in a Northern City.* New York: Harcourt, Brace, 1945.

Duncan, Beverly, Sabagh, Georges, and Van Arsdol, Maurice D., Jr. "Patterns of City Growth." *American Journal of Sociology* 67 (January 1962): 418-429.

Duncan, Otis Dudley. "After the Riots." *The Public Interest* 7 (Fall 1967):3-7.

_____. and Schnore, Leo. "Cultural, Behavioral, and Ecological Perspectives in the Study of Social Organization." *American Journal of Sociology* 65 (September 1959): 132-148.

Ecker, Grace Dunlop. *A Portrait of Old Georgetown.* Richmond: Garrett and Massie Incorporated, 1933.

Edwards, Ozzie. "Family Composition as a Variable in Residential Succession." *American Journal of Sociology* 77 (January 1972): 731-741.

Engels, Frederick. *The Condition of the Working Class in London in 1844.* 3rd Edition. London: Allen and Unwin, 1962.

Evening Star. 20 February 1948.

_____. 17 September 1949.

_____. 22 June 1950.

Farley, Reynolds. "Suburban Persistence." *American Sociological Review* 29 (February 1964): 38-47.

_____. and Taeuber, Karl E. "Population Trends and Residential Segregation since 1960." *Science* 159 (March 1968): 953-956.

Farley, Robert. "The Quality of Demographic Data for Non-Whites." *Demography* 5 (December 1968): 1-10.

Farrah, Morton. *Neighborhood Analyses.* New York: Chandler-Davis Publishing Company, 1969.

Fava, Sylvia. "Ecological Patterns Reviewed," in *Urbanism in World Perspective.* Edited by Sylvia Fava. New York: Thomas Y. Crowell Company, 1968.

Felson, Marcus. "Community and Debate." *American Journal of Sociology* 78 (December 1973): 674-676.

Firey, Walter. *Land Use in Central Boston.* Cambridge, Mass.: Harvard University Press, 1947.

First National Back to the City Conference. *Proceedings.* 1974.

Foote, Nelson N. *Housing Choices and Housing Constraints.* New York: McGraw-Hill, 1960.

Form, William H. "The Place of Social Structure in the Determination of Land

Use: Some Implications for a Theory of Urban Ecology." *Social Forces* 32 (May 1954): 317-323.

Form, William H., Smith, Joel, Stone, Gregory P., and Cowling, James. "The Compatibility of Alternative Approaches to the Delimitation of Urban Sub-Areas." *American Sociological Review* 19 (August 1954): 434-440.

Forman, Robert. *Black Ghettos, White Ghettos and Slums*. Englewood Cliffs, N.J.: Prentice-Hall, 1971.

Frieden, Bernard J. *The Future of Old Neighborhoods*. Cambridge, Mass.: MIT Press, 1964.

Gale, Dennis. "The Back-to-the-City Movement Revisited." Occasional Paper Series. Washington, D.C.: George Washington University, 1977.

Gans, Herbert. *The Urban Villagers*. New York: Free Press, 1962.

Gara, Larry. *The Liberty Line*. Lexington, Ky.: University of Kentucky Press, 1967.

Geer, Mary Warren. *How to Profit by Rehabilitation Real Estate*. Englewood Cliffs, N.J.: Prentice-Hall, Inc., 1957.

Gist, Noel P., Halbert, L.A. *Urban Society*. New York: Thomas Y. Crowell Company, 1948.

Glazer, Nathan. "Slum Dwellings Do Not Make a Slum." *New York Times Magazine* (November 1965), pp. 9-14.

Gordon, David M. *Problems in Political Economy: An Urban Perspective*. Lexington, Mass.: D.C. Heath and Company, 1971.

Green, Constance McLaughlin. *The Secret City*. Princeton, N.J.: Princeton University Press, 1967.

_____. *Washington: Village and Capitol 1800-1878*. Princeton, N.J.: Princeton University Press, 1962.

Grier, Eunice S. *Understanding Washington's Changing Population*. Washington, D.C.: Washington Center for Metropolitan Studies, 1961.

_____. and Grier, George. "Black Suburbanization at the Mid-1970's." Washington, D.C.: Washington Center for Metropolitan Studies, April 1978.

Grier, George, and Grier, Eunice. "Movers to the City." Washington, D.C.: Washington Center for Metropolitan Studies, 1977.

_____. *Equality and Beyond*. Chicago: Quadrangle Books, 1966.

Grieson, Ronald E. *Urban Economics*. Boston: Little, Brown and Comapny, 1971.

Guest, Avery M., and Zuiches, James J. "Commentary and Debate." *American Journal of Sociology* 78 (November 1973): 676-682.

Haig, Robert M. "Toward an Understanding of the Metropolis: The Assignment of Areas in Urban Regions." *Quarterly Journal of Economics* 40 (May 1926): 414-428.

Handlin, Oscar. *The Uprooted*. New York: Grosset and Dunlap, 1951.

Harrington, Michael. *The Other America: Poverty in the United States*. New York: Macmillan Company, 1962.

Hart, John Fraser. "The Changing Distribution of the American Negro," in *Black America*. Edited by Robert P. Ernest and Lawrence Hugg. New York: Anchor Books, 1976, pp. 49-70.

Hauser, Philip M. "Demographic Factors in the Integration of the Negro." *Daedalus* 94 (1965): 847-877.

Hawkes, Roland K. "Spatial Patterning of Urban Population Characteristics." *American Journal of Sociology* 78 (March 1973): 1216-1235.

Hawley, Amos H. *The Changing Shape of Metropolitan America: Deconcentration since 1920*. Chicago: University of Chicago Press, 1956.

_____. "Ecology and Human Ecology." *Social Forces* 12 (May 1944): 337-345.

_____. and Duncan, Otis D. "Social Area Analysis: A Critical Approach." *Land Economics* 53 (November 1957): 337-345.

Haynes, George Edmund. *The American Negro*. New York: Arno Press and *The New York Times*, 1969.

Helper, Rose. *Racial Policies and Practices of Real Estate Brokers*. Minneapolis: University of Minnesota Press, 1969.

Henri, Florette. *Black Migration*. New York: Doubleday Anchor, 1975.

Herron, Paul. *The Story of Capitol Hill*. New York: Coward McCann, 1963.

Holiday Magazine. February 1950, pp. 10-12.

Holt, Paul. "The Concept of the Natural Area." *American Sociological Review* 2 (November 1946): 423-427.

"Househunter's Guide." Family Housing Bureau, Chicago Title Insurance Company, Illinois, 1977.

Hoyt, Homer. "Recent Distortions of the Classical Models of Urban Structure." *Land Economics* 40 (May 1964): 199-212.

_____. *The Structure and Growth of Residential Neighborhoods in American Cities*. New York: Ronald Press, 1939.

Hunter, Floyd. *Community Power Structure: A Study of Decision Makers*. Chapel Hill, N.C.: University of North Carolina Press, 1953.

In Towner. Washington, D.C., December 1974.

_____. Washington, D.C., December 1975.

Jacobs, Jane. *The Death and Life of Great American Cities*. New York: Random House, 1961.

Jacoby, Susan. "Capitol Hill Integration Masks Conflicts." *New Republic* (January 1969), pp. 2-3.

Kantrowitz, Nathan. *Ethnic and Racial Segregation in the New York Metropolis*. New York: Praeger Publishers, 1973.

Kerner, Otto. *National Advisory Commission on Civil Disorders*. New York: Bantam Books, 1968.

Kreps, Juanita M. *Women and the American Economy: A Look into the 1980's*. American Assembly, Columbia University, 1976.

Loewenstein, Louis K., ed. *Urban Studies*. New York: Free Press, 1971.

"Look behind the Dirt and Find a Gold Mine." *House and Home* (October

1954), pp. 106-108.

Lynd, Staughton. "Urban Renewal—For Whom?" *Commentary* 31 (January 1961).

Mackall, S. Somervell. *Early Days of Washington*. Washington, D.C.: Peabody Collection, 1899.

Mandelker, Daniel R., and Montgomery, Roger. *Housing in America: Problems and Perspectives*. New York: Bobbs-Merrill Company, 1973.

McDermott, John, and Clark, Dennis. "Helping the Panic Neighborhood." *Interracial Review* 2 (August 1955): 30-38.

McEntire, Davis. *Residence and Race*. Berkeley, Calif.: University of California Press, 1960.

McKenzie, Roderick D. "The Ecological Approach." in *The City*. Edited by Robert E. Park, Ernest W. Burgess, and Roderick D. McKenzie. 4th Edition. Chicago: University of Chicago Press, 1967, pp. 63-79.

_____. *The Metropolitan Community*. New York: McGraw-Hill, 1933.

_____. "The Scope of Human Ecology," in *The Urban Community*. Edited by Ernest W. Burgess. Chicago: University of Chicago Press, 1925, pp. 151-172.

Means, Mary C. "Neighborhood Preservation Experiences." *A Midwestern Catalog* (September 1975), pp. 21-29.

Mercer, John. "Housing Quality and the Ghetto," in *Perspectives in Geography 2, Geography of the Ghetto*. Edited by Harold M. Rose. DeKalb, Ill.: Northern Illinois University Press, 1972, pp. 143-168.

Merton, Robert K. *Social Theory and Social Structure*. New York: Free Press, 1968.

Mields, Hugh, Jr. *Federally Assisted New Communities: New Dimensions in Urban Development*. Washington, D.C.: Urban Land Institute, 1973.

Molotch, Harvey. "The City as a Growth Machine: Toward a Political Economy of Place." *American Journal of Sociology* 82 (September 1976): 309-332.

_____. "Racial Integration in a Transitional Community." *American Sociological Review* 34 (December 1969): 878-893.

_____. "Reply to Guest and Zuiches: Another Look at Residential Turnover in Urban Neighborhoods." *American Journal of Sociology* 77 (November 1971): 468-471.

Moore, Carol. "Fixable Houses Downtown." *Money Magazine* (January 1974), pp. 17-25.

Moore, Charles. *Washington Past and Present*. New York: Century Company, 1929.

Mumford, Lewis. *The City in History: Its Origins, Its Transformation and Its Prospects*. New York: Harcourt, Brace and World, Inc., 1961.

Myrdal, Gunnar. *An American Dilemma*. New York: Harper and Row Publishers, 1944.

Nash, William. *Residential Rehabilitation: Private Profits and Public Purposes*. New York: McGraw-Hill, 1959.

National Observer. 15 December 1969.

"Neighborhood Diversity." *Hearings Before the Committee on Banking, Housing and Urban Affairs*, U.S. Senate, 95th Congress, July 7-8, 1977.

Nelson, Charmeynne D. "Myths about Black Women Workers in Modern America." *Black Scholar* (March 1975).

New York Times, 29 October 1972.

_____,18 November 1972.

_____, 11 June 1976.

_____, 20 June 1976.

_____, 13 July 1977.

Park, Robert. "The City: Human Behavior in the City Environment." *American Journal of Sociology* 20 (September 1915): 577-612.

Pettigrew, Thomas F. "Attitudes on Race and Housing: A Social Psychological View," in *Segregation in Residential Areas*. Edited by Amos H. Hawley and Vincent P. Rock. Washington, D.C.: National Academy of Sciences, 1973, pp. 21-84.

Preliminary Demographic Profile II. Urban Studies Program (typewritten). Washington, D.C.: Howard University, 1970.

"Racial Discrimination in the Private Housing Sector." *Maryland Law Review* 33 (1973): 289-291.

Reckler, Anita. "Private Renewal and Community Change." M.A. thesis, The George Washington University, 1974.

Report of the National Advisory Commission on Civil Disorders. Washington, D.C.: U.S. Government Printing Office, 1969.

Report of the National Association of Housing and Redevelopment. Washington, D.C.: U.S. Government Printing Office, 1974.

Report of the National Commission on Urban Problems: Building the American City. Washington, D.C.: U.S. Government Printing Office, 1968.

Report of the President's Committee on Urban Housing: A Decent Home. Washington D.C.: U.S. Government Printing Office, 1969.

Report of the United States Civil Rights Commission. Washington, D.C.: U.S. Government Printing Office, 1959.

Report to the District Committee on Finance and Revenue, April 1975.

Rose, Peter I. *The Subject is Race*. New York: Oxford University Press, 1968.

Rothman, Jack. "The Ghetto Makers," in *Housing Urban America*. Edited by Jon Pynoos, Robert Schafer, and Chester W. Hartman. Chicago: Aldine Publishing Company, 1973), pp. 274-278.

Saturday Evening Post. 20 March 1948.

Savitch, H.V. "Black Cities/White Suburbs: Domestic Colonialism as an Interpretive Idea." *Annals of the American Academy of Political and Social Science* (September 1978), pp. 118-134.

Schorr, Alvin L. "Housing the Poor," in *Urban Poverty: Its Social and Political Dimensions*. Edited by W. Bloomberg, Jr., and H.J. Schmandt. Beverly

Hills, Calif.: Sage Publications, 1970, pp. 53-75.

Schwirian, Kent P. *Comparative Urban Structure: Studies in the Ecology of Cities*. Lexington, Mass.: D.C. Heath and Company, 1974.

Second National Back to the City Conference. *Proceedings*, 1975.

Seig, Louis. "Concepts of Ghetto: A Geography of Minority Groups," in *Black America*. Edited by Robert T. Ernst and Lawrence Hugg. New York: Anchor Books, 1976, pp. 120-125.

Semenow, Robert W. *Questions and Answers on Real Estate*. Englewood Cliffs, N.J.: Prentice-Hall, 1962.

Shevky, Eshref and William Bell. *Social Area Analysis*. Stanford, Calif.: Stanford University Press, 1955.

_____. *Social Area Analysis: Theory, Illustrative Application and Computational Procedure*. Stanford, Calif.: Stanford University Press, 1955.

Shevky, Eshref, and Williams, Marilyn. *The Social Areas of Los Angeles*. Berkeley, Calif.: University of California Press, 1949.

Sjoberg, Gideon. "Comparative Urban Sociology," in *Sociology Today*. Edited by Robert K. Merton, Leonard Broom, and Leonard S. Cottrell, Jr. New York: Basic Books, 1959, pp. 334-359.

Smith, Joel. "A Method for the Classification of Areas on the Basis of Demographically Homogeneous Populations." *American Sociological Review* 19 (April 1954): 201-207.

"Special Report on Housing." *Miami Herald*, 5 August 1973.

Stanfield, Rochelle L. "Cities Being Rehabilitated Though Housing Ills Remain." *National Journal*, 17 July 1976.

Stanforth, Deirdre, and Stamm, Martha. *Buying and Renovating a House in the City*. New York: Alfred A. Knopf, 1972.

Stedman, Murray S., Jr. *Urban Politics*. Cambridge, Mass.: Winthrop Publishers, 1975.

Sternlieb, George, and Burchell, Robert. *Residential Abandonment: The Tenant Landlord Revisited*. New Brunswick, N.J.: Rutgers Center for Urban Policy Research.

Strauss, Anselm M. "The Latest in Urban Imagery," in *Internal Structure of the City*. Edited by Larry S. Bourne. New York: Oxford University Press, 1971, pp. 23-27.

_____. "Strategies for Discovering Urban Theory," in *Social Science and the City: A Survey of Research Methods*. Edited by Leo F. Schnore. New York: Frederick A. Praeger, 1968, pp. 78-102.

Struyk, Raymond J. *Urban Homeownership*. Lexington, Mass.: Lexington Books, D.C. Heath and Co., 1976.

Sweetser, Frank. "Factorial Ecology, Helsinki, 1960." *Demography* 2 (1965): 372-385.

Tabb, William K., and Sawers, Larry. *Marxism and the Metropolis*. New York: Oxford University Press, 1978.

Taeuber, Karl E., and Taeuber, Alma F. "The Negro as an Immigrant Group: Recent Trends in Racial and Ethnic Segregation in Chicago." *American Journal of Sociology* 69 (January 1964): 374-392.

_____. "White Migration and Socio-Economic Differences between Cities and Suburbs." *American Sociological Review* 29 (October 1964): 718-729.

Thomas, William I. "The Relation of Research to the Social Process," in *Essays on Research in the Social Sciences*. Edited by William I. Thomas. Washington, D.C.: The Brookings Institute, 1931, pp. 180-194.

Thrasher, Frederick M. *The Gang*. Chicago: University of Chicago Press, 1927.

Thursz, Daniel. "Where Are They Now?" Health and Welfare Council of the National Capital Area, 1969.

Times-Herald, 2 March 1945.

U.S. Bureau of the Census. "Financial Characteristics of the Housing Inventory." *Annual Housing Survey*. Washington, D.C.: U.S. Government Printing Office, 1974.

_____. *Metropolitan Housing Characteristics, United States and Regions*. Washington, D.C.: U.S. Government Printing Office, 1974.

U.S. Congress, Wadsworth Bill, 81st Congress, 1950. H.R. 10128.

U.S. Congress, Housing Act of 1954, 83rd Congress, 1954. H.R. 590.

U.S. Congress, Housing Act of 1958, 85th Congress, 1958. H.R. 1091.

U.S. Department of Commerce, Bureau of the Census. *Population and Housing Statistics for Census Tracts*. Washington, D.C.: U.S. Government Printing Office, 1942.

_____. *Population and Housing Statistics*. Washington, D.C.: U.S. Government Printing Office, 1950.

_____. *Population and Housing Statistics for Census Tracts*. Washington, D.C.: U.S. Government Printing Office, 1961.

_____. *Selected Population and Housing Charactersitics*. Washington, D.C.: U.S. Government Printing Office, 1970.

U.S. Department of Commerce. *Statistical Abstract of the United States*. Washington, D.C.: U.S. Government Printing Office, 1972.

U.S. Department of Housing and Urban Redevelopment. *Housing in the Seventies: A Report of National Housing Policy Review*. Washington, D.C.: U.S. Government Printing Office, 1974.

Vernon, Raymond. "The Economics and Finances of the Large Metropolis." *Daedalus* 90 (Winter 1961): 42-48.

Vidich, Arthur J., and Bensman, Joe. *Small Town in Mass Society*. Princeton, N.J.: Princeton University Press, 1959.

Vitchek, Norris. "Confessions of a Blockbuster." *Saturday Evening Post* (July 1962), pp. 15-19.

Walker, Mabel. *Urban Blight and Slums*. Cambridge, Mass.: Harvard University Press, 1938.

Wall Street Journal. 4 January 1976.

Washington Post. 5 May 1948.

_____, 20 Janaury 1969.

_____, 12 April 1972.

_____, 14 May 1974.

_____, 25 April 1975.

_____, 28 June 1975.

_____, 14 June 1976.

_____, 12 July 1976.

_____, 31 July 1976.

_____, 7 February 1978.

_____, 24 July 1978.

Washington Region 1974. "Population and Housing Data from Washington Area Census Updating System." Washington, D.C.: Center for Metropolitan Studies, 1974.

Weaver, Robert C. *The Negro Ghetto.* New York: Russell Press, 1948.

Weller, Charles Frederick. *Neglected Neighbors: Story of Life in the Alleys, Tenements and Shanties of the National Capitol.* Philadelphia: John C. Winston Co., 1909.

Wendt, Paul F. *Housing Policy—The Search for Solutions.* Berkeley, Calif.: University of California Press, 1962.

West, Alvin M. *The Future of Georgetown.* Washington, D.C.: Peabody Collection, May 1924.

Wheeler, Raymond. "The Relationship between Negro Invasion and Property Prices in Grand Rapids, Michigan." Ph.D. dissertation, University of Michigan, 1962.

White, Morton, and White, Lucia. *The Intellectual Versus the City.* Cambridge, Mass.: Harvard University Press, 1961.

Whyte, William F. *Street Corner Society.* Chicago: University of Chicago Press, 1943.

Wilcox, Preston. "Social Policy and White Racism." *Social Policy* 1 (May/June 1970): 41-46.

Wilson, James Q. "The Urban Unease: Community vs. the City." *The Public Interest* 12 (Summer 1968): 25-39.

Wilson, Robert A. "Anomie in the Ghetto: A Study of Neighborhood Type, Race and Anomie." *American Journal of Sociology* 77 (November 1971): 66-87.

Willheld, Sidney M. "The Concept of the 'Ecological Complex': A Critique." *American Journal of Economics and Sociology* 23 (July 1964): 241-248.

Winsborough, Hal H. "An Ecological Approach to the Theory of Suburbanization." *American Journal of Sociology* 68 (March 1963): 565-570.

Wirth, Louis. *On Cities and Social Life.* Chicago: University of Chicago Press, 1964.

_____. *The Ghetto.* Chicago: University of Chicago Press, 1928.

_____. "Urbanism as a Way of Life," in *Cities and Society*. Edited by Paul K. Hatt and Albert J. Reiss, Jr. New York: Free Press, 1951, pp. 46-63.

Wolf, Eleanor P. "On the Destruction of Poor Neighborhoods." *Social Problems* 15 (Summer 1967): 3-8.

_____. "The Tipping Point in Racially Changing Neighborhoods." *Journal of the American Institute of Planners* 29 (August 1963): 217-222.

_____. and Lebeaux, Charles N. *Change and Renewal in an Urban Community*. New York: Frederick A. Praeger, 1969.

Women and Poverty. Staff Report, U.S. Commission on Civil Rights, June 1976.

Wood, James Playsted. *Washington, D.C.* New York: Seabury Press, 1966.

Ziegler, Arthur P., Jr. *Historic Preservation in Inner City Areas*. Pittsburgh: Allegheny Press, 1971.

Index

About the Author

Eileen Zeitz is a National Science Foundation Postdoctoral Fellow working at the Center for Municipal and Metropolitan Research of the National Capital Area. Prior to this, she was an assistant professor in the sociology department at The George Washington University, teaching primarily in the urban learning graduate program. She has written and presented papers on various aspects of urban sociology, particularly in the area of housing.